SAVING ENDANGERED SPECIES

THE
GIANT
PANDA

Help Save This Endangered Species!

Alison Imbriaco

MyReportLinks.com Books

an imprint of

 Enslow Publishers, Inc.

Box 398, 40 Industrial Road
Berkeley Heights, NJ 07922
USA

Library of Congress Cataloging-in-Publication Data

Imbriaco, Alison.
  The giant panda : help save this endangered species! / Alison Imbriaco.
    p. cm.—(Saving endangered species)
  Includes bibliographical references and index.
  ISBN 1-59845-037-9
  1. Giant panda—Juvenile literature. I. Title. II. Series.
  QL737.C214I43 2006
  599.789—dc22

                                        2005031120

Printed in the United States of America

10 9 8 7 6 5 4 3 2 1

To Our Readers:
Through the purchase of this book, you and your library gain access to the Report Links that specifically
back up this book.

The Publisher will provide access to the Report Links that back up this book and will keep these Report
Links up to date on **www.myreportlinks.com** for five years from the book's first publication date.

We have done our best to make sure all Internet addresses in this book were active and appropriate when
we went to press. However, the author and the Publisher have no control over, and assume no liability
for, the material available on those Internet sites or on other Web sites they may link to.

The usage of the MyReportLinks.com Books Web site is subject to the terms and conditions stated on the
Usage Policy Statement on **www.myreportlinks.com**.

A password may be required to access the Report Links that back up this book. The password is found
on the bottom of page 4 of this book.

Any comments or suggestions can be sent by e-mail to comments@myreportlinks.com or to the address
on the back cover.

Photo Credits: © Corel Corporation, pp. 3, 29, 56, 81, 95; American Psychological Association, p. 103;
AnimalInfo.org, p. 59; ARKive, p. 37; China Giant Panda Museum, p. 94; China.org, p. 62; CITES, p. 78;
Enslow Publishers, Inc., p. 5; Environmental News Network, p. 15; Globio.org, p. 65; International
Network for Bamboo and Rattan, p. 53; IUCN, p. 76; Keren Su/China Span, pp. 10, 28, 39, 105; Library
of Congress, p. 22; Liu Bingsheng, AP/Wide World Photos, p. 70; Long Island University Library, p. 86;
Michigan State University, p. 41; MyReportLinks.com Books, p. 4; *National Geographic*.com, pp. 92, 101;
PBS, p. 45; Photos.com, pp. 1, 14, 17, 19, 31, 33, 48, 50, 52, 69, 98, 110; San Diego Zoo, p. 57;
Smithsonian National Zoological Park, pp. 43, 63, 91; The American Zoo and Aquarium Association,
pp. 75, 83; UNEP–WCMC, p. 100; UNESCO, p. 55; U.S. Fish and Wildlife Service, pp. 24, 113; World
Wildlife Fund, pp. 12, 107; World Wildlife Fund China, p. 109; Zoo Atlanta, p. 88.

Cover Photo: Keren Su/China Span.

CONTENTS

MyReportLinks.com Books
Great Books, Great Links, Great for Research!

The Internet sites featured in this book can save you hours of research time. These Internet sites—we call them **"Report Links"**—are constantly changing, but we keep them up to date on our Web site.

When you see this "Approved Web Site" logo, you will know that we are directing you to a great Internet site that will help you with your research.

Give it a try! Type http://www.myreportlinks.com into your browser, click on the series title and enter the password, then click on the book title, and scroll down to the Report Links listed for this book.

The Report Links will bring you to great source documents, photographs, and illustrations. MyReportLinks.com Books save you time, feature Report Links that are kept up to date, and make report writing easier than ever! A complete listing of the Report Links can be found on pages 114–115 at the back of the book.

Please see "To Our Readers" on the copyright page for important information about this book, the MyReportLinks.com Web site, and the Report Links that back up this book.

Please enter **SGP1969** if asked for a password.

Giant Panda
Range Map

MONGOLIA

CHINA

Panda Habitat
Cities
Provincial Boundaries
Nature Reserves

Huang He River

Lanzhou

GANSU

Xian

SHAANXI

WANGLANG
N.R.

TANGJIAHE
N.R.

QIANFOSHAN
N.R.

Chang Jiang River

WOLONG
N.R.

Chengdu

SICHUAN

YELE
N.R.

INDIA

MYANMAR

0   500 Miles

0   500 Kilometers

Giant Panda Facts

▶ **Class**
Mammalia

▶ **Order**
Carnivora

▶ **Family**
Ursidae

▶ **Genus and Species**
Ailuropoda melanoleuca (cat-footed black-and-white animal)

▶ **Chinese Names**
Huaxiong (banded bear), *xiongmao* (bearlike cat), and *daxiongmao* (great bear-cat)

▶ **Habitat**
Thick bamboo and coniferous forests above 8,000 feet (2,438 meters)

▶ **Range**
Mountains in the central and western Chinese provinces of Sichuan, Shaanxi, and Gansu

▶ **Wild Population**
Estimated to be 1,600 in 2005

▶ **Captive Population**
About 200

▶ **Average Length**
About 4 to 6 feet (1.2 to 1.8 meters)

▶ Height at Shoulder

27 to 32 inches (70 to 80 centimeters)

▶ Average Weight

220 to 330 pounds (100 to 150 kilograms). Males are about 10 percent larger than females.

▶ Gestation

Between 84 and 184 days

▶ Life Span

Unknown in the wild, but between 14 and 20 years in captivity

▶ Size at Birth

About 4 ounces (113 grams)

▶ Number of Young at Birth

One or two

▶ Age at Maturity

Females, 4 to 5 years; males, 6 to 7 years

▶ Diet

Giant pandas primarily eat bamboo, but they are omnivores.

▶ Status

Endangered

▶ Main Threats to Survival

Habitat loss; poaching; periodic bamboo shortages

Having transcended its mountain home to become a citizen of the world, the panda is a symbolic creature that represents our efforts to protect the environment.

George Schaller, *The Last Panda*

Chapter 1

IN LOVE WITH PANDAS

In 1972, United States president Richard Nixon visited China to begin official communications with that country. Diplomatic relations had not existed between the two countries for decades. Certainly the visit was an important political event. For the American people, though, the big news was that China would send two giant pandas to the United States as a gesture of friendship. The male and female pandas, Hsing-Hsing and Ling-Ling, found a new home at the Smithsonian National Zoological Park, more often known as the National Zoo, in Washington, D.C. There, an adoring public flocked to see them. Over the next twenty-eight years, an estimated 75 million people visited the zoo to see the pandas.[1]

▶ The Appeal of Pandas

Why are giant pandas so appealing? It may be that with their huge heads and roly-poly bodies, pandas look almost like overgrown teddy bears. Bowed front legs cause pandas to walk with a rolling, sailorlike gait, and they often tumble from trees or climbing structures without any indication

▲ *This giant panda cub in China's Wolong Reserve appears to be waving at the camera. Despite being one of the most recognizable and adored species on the planet, the giant panda is still critically endangered.*

of injury.[2] They seem funny, which they may be, and harmless, which they definitely are not. People even seem to enjoy watching pandas sleep and eat, which they do with their back legs stretched in front of them, using their forepaws to hold bamboo, the staple food in their diet.

Pandas are also distinctively marked, with black eye patches in large cream-colored faces and round, black ears. This black-and-white pattern extends to black "leggings" and a black band across their shoulders.

Part of the giant pandas' appeal may be simply that they are so rare. Fossils show that pandas once lived in many areas of eastern China and as far south as Vietnam. Today, wild giant pandas live only in the mountains of central China, in the Chinese provinces of Gansu, Shaanxi, and Sichuan. According to a recent Chinese government survey, about sixteen hundred giant pandas survive in the wild, and loss of habitat and poaching threaten their continued existence.[3]

The Pandas' World

The mountains that provide homes for giant pandas form a great arc that curves north and east to protect an area called the Sichuan Basin from extreme weather conditions. These mountains, including the Qinling Mountains to the north of the basin and the Min Mountains and Qionglai Mountains to the west, are much older than the Himalayas.[4] Since prehistoric times, they have protected the basin from cold winter storms and hot, dry summer winds sweeping across Asia. During the last ice age, the mountains stopped the spread of glaciers.

At the same time, the mountains catch the warm, moist air from the southeast. When this warm, moist air hits the mountains, it forms rain clouds. The result is a very wet, temperate climate, one without extremes of cold or hot weather. The Wolong Nature Reserve in these mountains, where many pandas live, receives an average of more than 50 inches (127 centimeters) of rain and snow each year.[5]

Many rare species survived the ice age in the protected temperate mountain climate on the eastern side of the Min and Qionglai mountains.

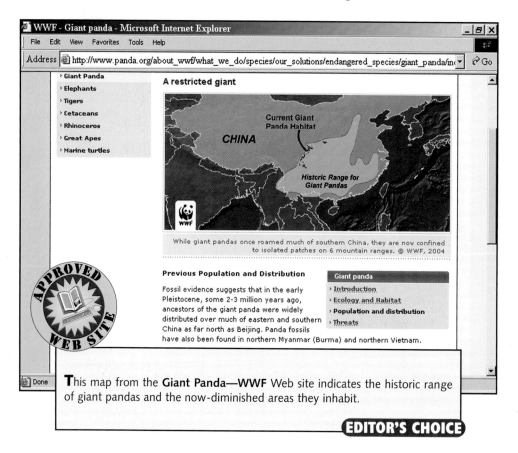

This map from the **Giant Panda—WWF** Web site indicates the historic range of giant pandas and the now-diminished areas they inhabit.

For example, one nature reserve in Sichuan, the Wolong Reserve, contains about ninety-three species of mammals and about four thousand species of plants. The Great Smoky Mountains National Park in the eastern United States, which is about the same size as Wolong, is home to about two thirds the number of mammal species and half the number of plant species.[6] Many of the species in China's central mountains exist nowhere else in the world. All the species living in this unusual area are threatened by loss of their habitat.

The Other Panda

The giant panda is not the only rare species in its homeland. It is not even the only panda. The red panda, a small raccoonlike animal, shares the giant panda's habitat. Cinnamon-red fur covers much of the red panda's body. Its legs and stomach are black, and rings of darker color mark its long, bushy tail. Pointed ears and white markings decorate its face.

Like its larger cousin, the red panda eats bamboo, but unlike the giant panda, the red panda adds berries, seeds, and acorns to its bamboo diet. And like the giant panda, the red panda is endangered. Red pandas share the giant panda's habitat in the mountains of central China, but they are also found in other parts of western and southern

▲ *The red panda, a distant cousin to the giant panda, is much smaller but also endangered.*

China as well as the Asian countries of Nepal, Bhutan, and Myanmar.

▶ What "Giant" Means

The giant panda might not be called giant if not for the red panda, or lesser panda. While adult red pandas weigh 10 to 15 pounds (5 to 7 kilograms), an adult black-and-white panda living in the wild usually weighs between 190 and 220 pounds (86 and 100 kilograms). Pandas living in zoos usually weigh more because food is provided for them. As far as bears go, however, giant pandas are not especially large. Brown bears and polar bears can weigh as much as 1,100 pounds (500 kilograms). Giant pandas are about 5 feet (1.5 meters) long, and their shoulder height is 27 to 32 inches (70 to 80 centimeters).[7]

China's National Treasure

The Chinese government recognized the giant panda's importance to Chinese culture in 1949 by designating it a national treasure. However, pandas have not figured prominently throughout China's long history. Many creatures, from tigers

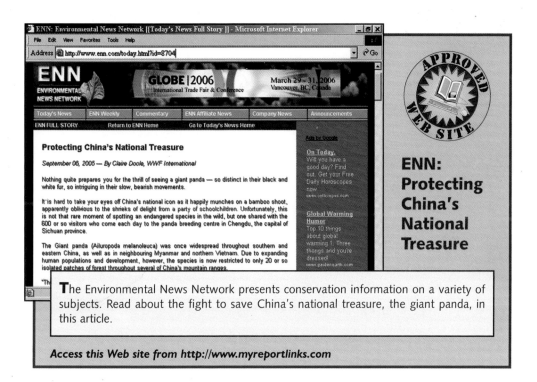

ENN: Protecting China's National Treasure

The Environmental News Network presents conservation information on a variety of subjects. Read about the fight to save China's national treasure, the giant panda, in this article.

Access this Web site from http://www.myreportlinks.com

and dragons to chickens and pigs, are named in the Chinese New Year cycle, but pandas are not. Unlike many other animals in China, pandas are not especially valued for medicinal use, and pandas rarely appeared in ancient Chinese art.

Still, Chinese history does mention the giant panda. Two early Chinese texts, one from between 770 and 256 B.C. and the other from about A.D. 100, refer to the *mo,* a black-and-white bear-like animal that ate metal. The reputation as a metal-eating bear probably comes from pandas' occasional trips to villages where they licked metal cooking pots. With teeth strong enough to chew tough bamboo stems, pandas can chew up pots to get at food remains. Ancient Chinese history also mentions that a panda was buried with a Chinese empress and that an emperor's garden contained rare animals of which the panda was the most treasured.[8]

Discovery

The giant panda was not known to the Western world until 1869, when a French priest named Père Armand David first saw a panda skin in the home of a wealthy Chinese landowner. Père David had worked as a Jesuit missionary in China since 1862, and, while there is no record of the number of people he converted, his discoveries of rare plants and animals are well known.

▲ *Bamboo is the primary diet of the giant panda.*

During his years in China, the priest made several trips to collect specimens, which he then sent to France. One of these trips took him to an area near the mountains along the Tibetan border. In March 1869, less than two weeks after Père David first saw a panda skin, hunters brought him a recently killed young panda and then an adult female. The priest sent the pandas to the Paris Museum of Natural History, noting that they were "the prettiest kind of animal" he had seen.[9]

▶ Are Pandas Raccoons or Bears?

Père David thought his discovery was a kind of bear. When the panda specimens arrived in Paris, though, the scientist who studied them noticed some similarities to the red panda, which had been discovered almost eighty years earlier by a Dutch botanist. The red panda resembles a raccoon. For more than a century, scientists debated whether or not the two pandas are closely related and whether they are members of the raccoon family, the bear family, or a separate panda family.

The giant panda looks like a bear; the red panda looks like a raccoon. What the two pandas have in common is a diet of bamboo, and both species have adapted to that diet, so their teeth, skulls, and forepaws are similar. But are they related? Recently, scientists have been able to study the molecules that make up the animals, including the molecules that carry hereditary material (DNA). Even after these highly scientific and technical studies had been conducted, scientists still had no definitive answer.[10]

▲ A bear or a raccoon? Scientists have long debated just what kind of animal the giant panda is, but recent DNA studies have led them to conclude the species is part of an evolutionary line that led to bears.

Recently, however, based on studies of genes, scientists have concluded that both pandas are branches of an evolutionary line that led eventually to bears. Red pandas diverged from this branch about 60 million years ago, following raccoons by a few million years. About 18 million years ago, the black-and-white panda separated from the branch, a few million years before other species of bear became distinct.[11]

▶ Su Lin

By the beginning of the nineteenth century, word of the unusual black-and-white bear had spread, and hunters decided it was a trophy they must have. Giant pandas were probably rare even then and, as researchers later found, particularly good at staying out of sight. Scientific and hunting expeditions alike were not successful. In 1916, a Westerner claimed to have seen a live panda. The next sighting was in 1929, when two sons of former United States president Theodore Roosevelt became the first Westerners to shoot a panda.

In 1935, a wealthy American named William Harkness went to China to capture a panda, but he died before he could find one. Shortly before Harkness left for China, he had married, and when his wife, Ruth, learned of her husband's death, she decided to fulfill his quest. Within months, Ruth Harkness arrived in what is now the Wolong

Reserve. Soon after she arrived, her camp overseer, Quentin Young, found a baby panda in a tree. With great foresight, Ruth Harkness had brought a baby bottle and dried milk with her, and she was able to care for the young panda and keep it alive.

The panda cub, named Su Lin, arrived in San Francisco in December 1936. Ruth Harkness intended to present Su Lin to the New York Zoological Society —for a large fee. However, officials there worried about the bowed legs and toes pointing inward that give pandas their special gait. The officials refused to take the cub because they were afraid she was not healthy.[12] The National Zoo in Washington, D.C., also decided not to take Su Lin; the price was too high.[13] Su Lin finally found a home at the Brookfield Zoo in Chicago, but she died about fifteen months later from pneumonia.

In Love With Pandas

Su Lin had been the beginning of an American love affair with the giant panda. In the early 1900s, at least forty-two dead giant pandas were taken out of China.[14] After Su Lin arrived in the United States, the hunting of pandas for museums came to an end. Zoo directors saw Su Lin's popularity and wanted live pandas. Hunters continued to pursue giant pandas to capture the animals for zoos.

In the 1930s, Su Lin, the first panda cub brought to the United States, found a home at Chicago's Brookfield Zoo. This poster from the zoo celebrated the unusual black-and-white bear, hoping to attract visitors. Unfortunately, Su Lin survived for less than two years.

By 1939, the Sichuan provincial government issued a decree to stop the capture of pandas, but it was largely ignored. Between 1937 and 1946, fourteen giant pandas reached foreign zoos.[15] The number of pandas that died before arriving on foreign soil is not known. In 1949, when the People's Republic of China was formed by the Communist government, China closed its borders. The drain on the panda population from outside sources came to an end.

Endangered

Between 2000 and 2004, China's State Forestry Administration and the environmental organization known as the World Wildlife Fund studied an 8,880-square-mile area (nearly 23,000 square kilometers) in the Chinese provinces of Sichuan, Shaanxi, and Gansu. The study used computer and satellite technologies to locate pandas and learn about their habitat.

The census indicated that 1,590 pandas live in China's mountain forests. An earlier survey had counted only about eleven hundred wild pandas.[16] The larger number in 2004 does not mean, however, that the panda population has increased. By 2004, the survey techniques to count pandas had improved.

The four-year study also revealed that pandas are still at risk because their habitat continues to

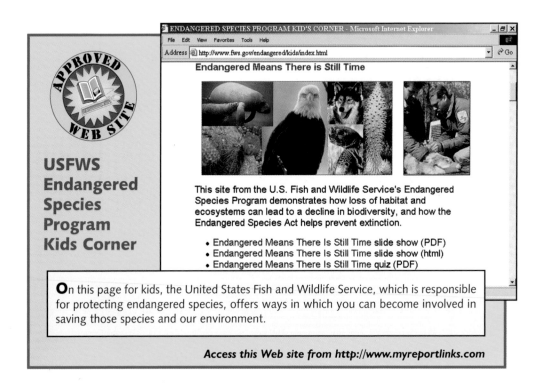

**USFWS
Endangered
Species
Program
Kids Corner**

ENDANGERED SPECIES PROGRAM KID'S CORNER - Microsoft Internet Explorer

File   Edit   View   Favorites   Tools   Help

Address http://www.fws.gov/endangered/kids/index.html   Go

Endangered Means There is Still Time

This site from the U.S. Fish and Wildlife Service's Endangered Species Program demonstrates how loss of habitat and ecosystems can lead to a decline in biodiversity, and how the Endangered Species Act helps prevent extinction.

- Endangered Means There Is Still Time slide show (PDF)
- Endangered Means There Is Still Time slide show (html)
- Endangered Means There Is Still Time quiz (PDF)

On this page for kids, the United States Fish and Wildlife Service, which is responsible for protecting endangered species, offers ways in which you can become involved in saving those species and our environment.

Access this Web site from http://www.myreportlinks.com

disappear. Humans' use of the forests has divided panda habitat into small fragments. Unless the fragments are connected, pandas may soon be extinct in the wild.

▷ What You Can Do to Save Giant Pandas

Although wild giant pandas live only in small areas of central China, people around the world are working to help the species survive. You can help, too.

You are already taking the first step toward helping to protect this endangered species by learning about it. As you learn more about pandas and their home in China, share what you learn with the adults around you. Discuss conservation problems to help them understand the needs of endangered species around the world. For example, you and your parents could learn more about the products your family uses. If your family is considering new furniture, check to be sure the wood used to make the furniture does not come from forests that are home to endangered species. Once forest habitat is lost, all the animals that depend upon the forest for their survival will suffer.

Other Ways to Get Involved

Another adult you can talk to is your teacher. If your class or your school participates in fund-raising projects, find out about Adopt-a-Panda programs, which are available through several conservation organizations, including the World Wildlife Fund, the Oakland China Wildlife Preservation Foundation, the National Zoo, and several other zoos.

Visit a zoo close to you, and find out how the zoo is involved in the protection of endangered species. Only a few zoos in North America—those in San Diego, Atlanta, Washington, D.C., and Memphis—have pandas, but other zoos are conducting research that may help giant pandas survive. The larger zoos with Web sites are only a mouse-click away. At the zoo closest to you, ask them about any ongoing research to help pandas and other endangered animals.

You may think of other creative ways to help the environment and endangered species. To find ideas that might spark your imagination, visit Aza's Web, a Web site of the American Zoo and Aquarium Association (AZA). This Web site describes what young people are doing to help endangered species.

Chapter 2 ▶

THE GRASS-EATING BEARS

A cloud rests on the mountain peak, silently dripping moisture on the high alpine meadow. As it descends the mountain, the cloud drenches the dense green forest below the meadow. Shapes—a tall fir tree, a small deer—loom darkly in the mist and then disappear as the fog closes around them. Wisps of cloud drift into the valley below the mountain's steep slopes until the mountain seems suspended. This, the world of the giant panda, is often a strange and eerie one.

In the high cloud-draped mountains of China, many of the animals seem to have stepped from the pages of a fairy tale. Orange monkeys with thick manes and blue "masks" around their eyes scamper through branches. Temminck's tragopan, pheasants with blue faces, rustle in the under-brush. And odd-looking takin, mammals related to goats and musk ox, browse on the forest under-growth. The renowned zoologist George Schaller, who has studied pandas, mountain gorillas, and lions, among other animals, described takin as having the "bulky, humped body of a brown bear,

This cub clings to a tree silhouetted against the mist-shrouded mountains of Wolong.

▲ *This panda, head held low, strikes a threatening pose.*

the legs of a cow, . . . the knobby horns of a wilde-beest, and the black, bulging face of a moose with mumps."[1]

Next to their exotic neighbors, the black-and-white pandas seem almost ordinary. Yet the panda is a very unusual animal. It presents scientists with one puzzle after another. One question that zoologists ask is why pandas have the distinctive black-and-white pattern. Sometimes an animal's coloring serves as camouflage to help it blend in with its environment. In fact, the black-and-white pattern does make a panda difficult to see in the snow. However, in the mountains where pandas live, snow covers the ground only a few months of the year. Pandas spend most of their time in thick clumps of green bamboo.

George Schaller theorized that the giant panda's coloring is black and white not to hide it but to make it easy to see. Pandas prefer to spend their days away from other pandas. When they can easily see other pandas in the green forest, they can choose paths away from their own kind.

The black eye patches and black ears also evolved to allow pandas to communicate with other pandas, according to Schaller's theory. Among many animals, stares are threatening. Animals may try to outstare a rival rather than actually fight it. A panda's eye patches make its small eyes look enormous—and make the stare more threatening. It is interesting, as Schaller noted, that an appearance that people find cuddly may have evolved to make pandas look more threatening to other pandas. When pandas use their stares to threaten, they hold their heads low. The black ears above black eye patches look almost like a second set of staring eyes. Schaller noticed that when a panda does not want to appear aggressive, it may cover its eye patches with its paws or hide its face.[2]

Bamboo

Just as puzzling as a panda's appearance is its diet. Pandas in the wild spend almost all of their time eating bamboo, a kind of grass with hollow, woody stems. Berries, meat, and plants other than

▲ *Although bamboo is plentiful in the pandas' habitat, the animals must eat a lot of it to get the proper nutrition.*

bamboo make up about one percent of all that pandas consume. Scientists believe that giant pandas have been living on their bamboo diet for 3 million years.[3]

One advantage of bamboo is that the pandas can almost always find plenty of it to eat within established ranges. Bamboo is green all year; pandas munch on the stems and leaves even when snow covers the ground. Bamboo is the fastest growing plant on Earth; some species of bamboo grow to a height of more than 100 feet (30 meters).[4]

But the loss of bamboo forests to development is the primary reason for the panda's decline.

▶ Favorite Grasses

Pandas living in the wild choose to eat only a few of the many species of bamboo growing in their mountains. One favorite is umbrella bamboo, which often grows on the lower slopes of the mountains at altitudes below 8,000 feet (2,400 meters). Slender stems less than half an inch (1 centimeter) thick usually grow to a height of 8 feet (2.5 meters), although they can grow to twice that height. Arrow bamboo, another panda favorite, grows at higher altitudes, from 8,500 feet to 10,500 feet (2,600 meters to 3,200 meters). Arrow bamboo stems are usually less than one fifth of an inch in diameter, and they grow to a height of about 4.5 feet (1.4 meters).[5]

Most grasses grow from seeds spread by grass that died during the winter. Bamboo does not die each winter. Instead, it grows from underground rootlike stems called rhizomes. The rhizomes spread underground and send up new shoots each spring. From time to time, the bamboo plants in an area flower and die all at once, spreading millions of seeds. This mass die-off may happen once every several years or once in a hundred years, depending on the type of bamboo.

A Strange Diet

While the bamboo itself is plentiful, it does *not* give pandas plenty of nutrition. Bamboo stalks consist of thick cell walls that are not easy to digest. Inside the tough cells walls are small amounts of easily digested nutrients in the form

The digestive system of pandas makes it difficult for them to digest their primary food—bamboo.

of starches and proteins. Because the cell walls in grass are not easy to digest, most herbivores, animals that eat grass, have specialized digestive systems. Extended intestines or stomachs with separate compartments hold the grass for a longer time, and special bacteria cause the plant's cell walls to ferment and break down so the nutrients can be digested.

Difficult to Digest

Unfortunately, pandas do not have the extended intestines or digestive bacteria that other grass eaters have. Pandas' digestive systems resemble the digestive systems of omnivores such as bears, who eat fruit, seeds, and meat, and carnivores such as cats, who eat meat. A panda's intestine is five to seven times the length of its body. By comparison, a cat's intestine is about four times the length of its body, a horse's intestine is about ten times its body length, and a cow's intestine is twenty times its body length.[6]

Because pandas have the digestive system of omnivores or carnivores, they digest a very small portion—only about 17 percent—of the bamboo they eat. According to Schaller, deer digest about 80 percent of the grass they eat. Lions digest about 90 percent of their dinner of meat.[7] Most of what pandas eat is useless bulk that passes through their digestive systems without providing nutrition.

▶ Quantity Over Quality

To get enough nutrition, pandas need to spend as much as fourteen to sixteen hours a day eating

American Embassy: Panda Primer

Access this Web site from http://www.myreportlinks.com

The American Embassy in China issued a page of facts about giant pandas, including panda distribution, issues of captivity, panda-for-rent programs, and the politics behind conservation. Read this paper at the embassy's Web site.

bamboo. As Schaller watched a wild panda one wintry day, he counted the year-old stems and leaves the animal ate. Based on this count, Schaller calculated that the panda ate parts of about twenty-two hundred stems as well as leaves from about fourteen hundred stems. The zoologist estimated that the panda ate 31 pounds (14 kilograms) of bamboo in the twenty-four-hour period.[8] Larger pandas might eat as much as 40 pounds (18 kilograms) in a day.

Although pandas do not digest their food efficiently, they are very good at consuming it. They often sit, leaning against a stump or rock, so they can use the sharp claws on their forepaws to grasp a bamboo stem, bend it, and bite it off close to the ground. Pandas are able to grasp slender bamboo stalks because they have radial sesamoids, "thumbs" that are actually enlarged wrist bones. After biting off bamboo stems and sniffing them to be sure they are good, pandas push them into their mouths as they quickly bite and chew. As they bite, they jerk the stem up and down and, at the same time, nod their heads up and down to make the biting more effective. The pandas swallow a mouthful of bamboo after a few quick chews.[9]

Bamboo stems are tough, but pandas have the teeth and muscles they need to bite off pieces of stem and chew the tough mouthfuls. Pandas' round heads are a result of their strong jaws and muscles. A curved bone (sagittal crest) above the brain combines with wide cheekbones to form an almost perfect circle. These bones are needed to support the animal's powerful jaw muscles. The panda's teeth behind its strong canines are larger than the teeth of other bears. These larger teeth, more like human molars than the teeth of other carnivores, are necessary for grinding the bamboo.

Shoots and Stems

In the spring, pandas add juicy bamboo shoots to their diet. Sitting, pandas use their forepaws to quickly peel the husk from a shoot before eating it. As George Schaller fed shoots to a captive panda, he noted that it took the panda an average of thirty-seven seconds to peel and eat a bamboo shoot. Later, he estimated that a wild female panda ate 84 pounds (38 kilograms) of bamboo shoots in a twenty-four-hour period. She needed to eat that many shoots to get nutrition because bamboo shoots, although the part of the plant highest in calories, are also 90 percent water.[10]

Counting Calories

Even with this, however, pandas are barely able to eat enough food to get the calories they need. Schaller calculated that pandas consume 4,300 to 4,500 calories a day and that they probably use about four thousand calories a day in normal activities.[11] Because of their choice of food, he speculated, pandas have little energy to spare.

Giant panda female with young

ARKive is a unique global program whose mission is to gather and display images and recordings of the world's endangered species. Movies and still images of the giant panda are available at **ARKive: Giant Panda**.

EDITOR'S CHOICE

Schaller also thought that conserving energy may have set the ground rules for panda society, although there has never been a detailed study of pandas' energy levels. In their mountain habitat, pandas live solitary lives. It is possible that pandas have chosen to avoid one another rather than fight over territory. However, pandas do communicate with other pandas. They may huff, snort, and chomp to indicate that they are uneasy or ready to attack. When they do attack, they roar. Giant pandas honk when they are distressed, and they squeal when threatened. A bleating noise is friendly.[12]

Keeping Warm

The bamboo that pandas prefer today only grows high in the mountains, at elevations of 6,600 feet (2,012 meters) and more. Giant pandas often spend their days at elevations above 8,500 feet (2,951 meters). At these high elevations, the temperature can be cold. To keep them warm, pandas have a coat of short, thick fur. They even have hair on the bottoms of their feet. The fur is slightly oily, which helps to keep the pandas dry in their damp habitat.

Pandas' fur does such a good job of keeping them warm that they can fall asleep sitting in the snow and not feel the cold. Pandas do not build nests for sleeping; they are more likely to fall

The giant panda's thick fur helps to keep it warm even in the cold, snowy mountains where it makes its home.

asleep wherever they have been eating. Zoologists speculate that pandas evolved to their present size in order to retain more body heat without using too much energy. (A larger body has relatively less surface area where body heat is lost.)

Scent Marking

Most often, pandas communicate by leaving scent and claw markings on trees. Male and female pandas have scent glands under their short, bushy tails. They usually hold their tails close to their bodies. When they want to leave a "calling card" on a tree, they use their tails as brushes to wipe the surface with secretions from the gland. Males sometimes add a squirt of urine and sometimes "walk" their back legs up the tree so that they are doing a handstand to mark it, while females seem to prefer highly placed marks, according to some scientific studies.

As Schaller followed a panda's tracks one day, he found that the panda marked one in every twelve trees it passed. In a three-day period, in which it averaged three-quarters of a mile of travel each day, the panda marked forty-five trees.[13]

The scent markings leave information, including the age, sex, and identity of the panda that left the scent.[14] When pandas investigate scents, they lick and sniff. They curl back their upper lip as they inhale to get the scent to a vomeronasal

A group of researchers from Michigan State University traveled to China to study the effects that humans are having on the natural habitat of the giant panda. Read more about their research on this Web site.

Access this Web site from http://www.myreportlinks.com

organ through tiny openings behind their teeth. This organ helps them interpret smells. (Humans do not have a vomeronasal organ, although most mammals do.)[15]

Usually, male pandas are the ones to leave scent markings, which are sniffed by females. Female pandas do leave scent markings during mating season, however, to attract males. Males check the scent posts for information about females and about other males they might compete with for the females. Although scent markings help pandas find one another at mating time, pandas use the markings during the rest of the year to avoid each other.

▶ Courting

Pandas do need to spend some time together in order to produce young pandas. Once a year, usually between mid-March and mid-May, females are in heat, or estrus, the period in which they are most likely to become pregnant. During the few days that they are in estrus, females are courted by males in the area and may mate with several of them. The males spend much of their time during these days tussling and roaring at each other to demonstrate their strength and assert their status.

Gestation, the time the female carries the fertilized egg, may last from 84 to 184 days through a process called delayed implantation.[16] This process allows the fertilized eggs to float in the mother's uterus until conditions seem right for their growth. The delay may be one month or as much as four months. Conditions that determine when the egg begins to develop may include temperature, exposure to light, and the availability of food. It is possible that if conditions remain poor, the fertilized egg never develops.[17]

Before giving birth, female pandas find a suitable place for a den. For some, the first choice is a large, hollow tree. In areas where the large trees have been cut down, pregnant females seem to prefer caves. An important consideration in den choice is a nearby source of water so mothers

Giant Panda Cub Photo Gallery: August 30 - National Zoo| FONZ - Microsoft Internet Explorer

File   Edit   View   Favorites   Tools   Help

Address http://nationalzoo.si.edu/Animals/GiantPandas/MeetPandas/PandaCubGallery/5.cfm   Go

Smithsonian
National Zoological Park | Friends of
                              the National 🐾   [search]

Visit | Animals, etc. | About Us | Activities & Events | Conservation & Science | Education | Publications | Join FONZ | Support the Zoo | Shop

Giant Pandas

Home |...| Giant Pandas | Meet the Zoo's Giant Pandas | Panda Cub Gallery

Giant Panda Cub Photo Gallery

Panda Cub Gallery

Thumbnails
Get Cub Wallpaper When You
Support the Giant Panda
Conservation Fund
Panda Cub Updates
Meet Mei Xiang & Tian Tian
Panda Photo Gallery
Giant Pandas for Kids
Giant Panda Facts
Panda Cub Development
Frequently Asked Cub
Questions
Panda Cams

Related Resources

On August 25, the cub opened his eyes and was even cuter than before. He had his fourth exam on August 30, and weighed 6.2 pounds. Staff could not get a total body length because he squirmed so much.

The **Smithsonian National Zoological Park** is home to three giant pandas, including a cub born in 2005. At the zoo's Web site, read about the zoo's pioneering work in panda conservation, view images of pandas, and learn more about how you can help save the species.

EDITOR'S CHOICE

can drink without leaving the infant for long. Mothers may partially cover the den's entrance with brush or saplings.

Panda Cubs

Although the average length of pregnancy is 138 days, the actual development of the egg is short, often only 50 to 60 days.[18] Infant pandas are born in a very undeveloped stage. They are about the size of a stick of butter and weigh only about 4 to 6 ounces (120 to 175 grams), making them the smallest baby mammals (except for kangaroos and opossums) relative to their mother's size. Newborns are blind and toothless. Their pink bodies have a thin cover of white hair. When they are first born, the infants look nothing like adult pandas.

The females give birth to one or two infants. When twins are born in the wild, it is rare that both survive—the mother will care more for one than the other, to ensure that at least one survives. Infant pandas are completely helpless at birth, except for one thing. They have a loud, penetrating squawk, which they use to tell their mother that something is wrong. Considering that the infant panda is about 0.12 percent of the mother's weight, the loud cry is important.[19]

A study of captive panda mothers showed that throughout the first weeks of the infant's life, the mother holds its infant close about 80 percent of the time.[20] The tiny baby disappears from view under the mother's forepaw. Without a warm coat, the infant needs its mother's warmth, and it suckles, or nurses, often.

▶ Growing Up

By the end of the third week, the baby panda has fur with panda markings and looks like a miniature adult. It is still completely dependent on its mother, though. The infant's eyes are barely open at the age of five to six weeks. At seven weeks, the

The San Diego Zoo was responsible for the birth of Hua Mei, one of the few panda cubs to be born and survive in captivity. Read more about the birth on *Nature: Bamboo Bears,* a PBS Web site.

EDITOR'S CHOICE

panda cub can lift its head and begins to crawl. It will not walk until it is four to five months old. At about three months of age, the panda cub begins to get teeth, but it will not begin to eat bamboo until its teeth are strong enough to crush the stalks.

As panda cubs grow, their mothers spend more time play-fighting, or engaging in rough play, with them.[21] By the time that panda cubs are thirteen to fourteen months old, they weigh about eighty pounds (thirty-six kilograms) and, like their mothers, are living entirely on bamboo.

Cubs stay with their mothers for another year or two before striking out on their own to find a territory. Female cubs usually travel farther to find a suitable habitat without other females. Female pandas are mature at four to five years of age. Males are mature at six to seven years.

Scientists are not certain how long wild pandas live. In zoos and breeding centers, pandas usually live fourteen to twenty years, although some live much longer. The National Zoo's Hsing-Hsing lived to be twenty-eight years old, and several pandas in Chinese zoos lived to be more than thirty years old.

Chapter 3

AN UNCERTAIN FUTURE

The lands where giant pandas live do not seem, on the surface, to be places that most people would find desirable. Still, habitat loss is the greatest threat to the pandas' ability to survive. Pandas live high in rugged mountains with steep, forbidding slopes. The black-and-white bears slip quietly through thick forest growth that people find nearly impassable. For thousands of years, the rugged mountains protected the giant panda's privacy. In the last century or so, demand for land and for the forests' resources have changed the mountain landscapes—and reduced the pandas' numbers.

▶ The Red Basin

When people first arrived in the Sichuan Basin more than two thousand years ago, the land was forested. As people cleared the trees for farmland, they found rich red soil, and the area became known as the Red Basin. Through the centuries, the area's good soil and moderate temperatures have allowed farmers to harvest crops as often as

▲ As China becomes less rural and more industrialized, the pandas' habitat is disappearing.

three times a year. Rain falls frequently in the mountains along the edge of the Red Basin, and in the past, the forests held the water in the soil so that it drained into the basin in clear mountain streams.

Farmers planted rice, wheat, and fruit trees and went into the mountain forests for medicinal herbs and bamboo. (Bamboo is used as a building material, and people as well as pandas eat the tender bamboo shoots.) People also took wood from the forest to use in construction and as fuel.

The population of the Red Basin increased steadily, but farmers could not turn mountainsides into farmland because rice and wheat do not grow at high altitudes. Then during the 1500s, traders brought New World crops to China. Corn, chili peppers, and potatoes will grow at higher altitudes and in poor soil. Farmers began to cut trees to clear terraces on the mountainsides and plant the new crops. By the end of the 1700s, corn had become the most important food crop in southwestern China.[1]

Loss of Forests

The new crops may be one reason for the tremendous increase in the population of Sichuan Province. More people meant more trees were cut to clear farmland, and farmers cut still more trees for fuel. Sometimes, farmers who took animals to graze in mountain meadows destroyed trees from above. They used fire to widen the meadows, and these fires sometimes spread into the forests.

As the population throughout China grew, demand for timber to use in construction also increased. Across China, forests disappeared. Looking for timber, logging companies ventured onto the steep mountain slopes, building roads and planting corn to feed employees. The rugged mountains no longer protected the pandas from intruders. Conservationists estimate that between

As the demand for timber grows, trees like this one become more scarce in the pandas' mountain home. The forests of China's central provinces have been decimated in the past thirty years.

the mid-1970s and the mid-1980s, loggers reduced the forests that provided habitat for the giant panda by 50 percent.[2] According to the World Wildlife Fund, the forests of China's central provinces once covered about 300,000 square miles (777,000 square kilometers). Today only about 83,000 square miles (215,000 square kilometers) are forested.[3]

Floods

Clearing steep mountainsides of trees endangers people as well as pandas, since flooding becomes a threat each time it rains. This was the case in the Red Basin, as forests disappeared from the mountains. Instead of rainwater draining into the basin year-round, rainwater spilled into it, causing rivers to overflow. At other times of the year, mountain streams dried up.

In 1998, floods in the Red Basin killed more than three thousand people and caused about $30 billion in damage. Almost immediately after the flood, the Chinese government ordered logging companies to stop cutting trees in the mountains. The government budgeted more than $2 billion for forest conservation throughout China, and loggers were paid to plant trees instead of cutting them down.[4]

However, trees are still being cut: Local people still use wood for fuel, and on a larger scale, the

▲ Habitat loss poses the greatest threat to endangered species. Although conservation has helped to preserve some of the giant pandas' forest habitat, logging is still affecting the species.

Chinese government cuts trees as it builds dams for hydroelectric plants. In addition, the reforestation program called Grain for Green may not accomplish what it was intended to accomplish. In many places, people planted trees, such as fruit trees, to provide an income. But clearing the native growth to plant these trees may defeat their purpose as flood control, and fruit trees do not provide the proper environment for bamboo to grow.

One small example of the demand for wood is disposable wooden chopsticks. An estimated 25 million trees per year are turned into about 45 billion pairs of disposable chopsticks. One province in China has taken the step of banning the production and sale of the disposable chopsticks.[5]

Feeling the Squeeze

As suitable panda habitat is lost to farmers, loggers, and hydroelectric plants, fewer pandas can find the privacy and food they need. Pandas eat bamboo that grows in the shade of old conifer trees. When logging companies cut all the trees in an area, a procedure known as clear-cutting, the shade-loving bamboo cannot grow in that area.

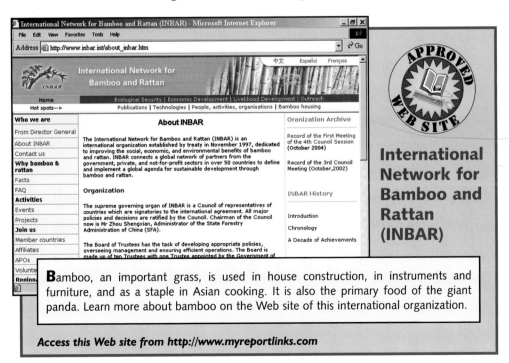

Bamboo, an important grass, is used in house construction, in instruments and furniture, and as a staple in Asian cooking. It is also the primary food of the giant panda. Learn more about bamboo on the Web site of this international organization.

Access this Web site from http://www.myreportlinks.com

Individual pandas do not need great expanses of suitable habitat. Pandas travel short distances each day, and their entire home ranges are small. Pandas in the Wolong Nature Reserve use only about 1.5 to 2.5 square miles (3.9 to 6.4 square kilometers).[6] While pandas do not need large territories, they choose their habitat carefully. They prefer gentle slopes and a mostly shady environment.[7]

Pandas also need privacy in their home territories. Female pandas do not share home ranges. Even so, the available panda habitat could probably support enough pandas to make survival of the species possible—if the available habitat existed in one large area.

The Danger of Inbreeding

Although conservationists have not determined exactly how many individuals in a species are necessary for the species' health, they usually estimate that a species' long-term survival requires at least five hundred individuals. A population with fewer than five hundred will most likely show the effects of inbreeding, related individuals mating and producing young. Inbreeding results in harmful changes in the species' gene pool. (Genes are the tiny units of inherited characteristics carried on chromosomes.) Harmful characteristics show up more often in inbred groups, resulting in individuals with less strength and energy. Inbreeding can also mean that fewer infants survive. In addition, the smaller gene pool means fewer of the genes not absolutely necessary for survival will be passed on. While such genes are not necessary in one generation, absence of the genes makes the species less able to adapt to change over time.

Fragmented Habitat

As farmers and logging companies cleared land of trees, they looked for level places, which are often

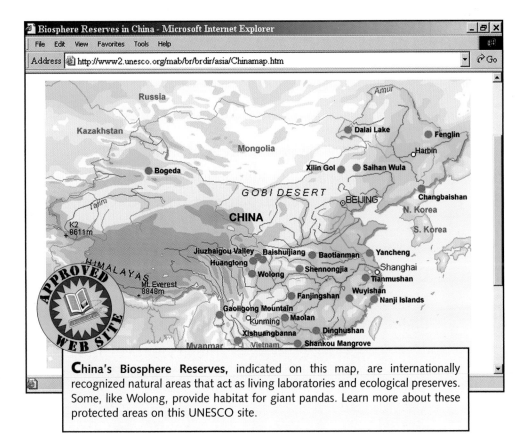

China's Biosphere Reserves, indicated on this map, are internationally recognized natural areas that act as living laboratories and ecological preserves. Some, like Wolong, provide habitat for giant pandas. Learn more about these protected areas on this UNESCO site.

▲ *Trekking in the snowy mountains of Sichuan Province. The key to saving pandas is getting people and pandas to coexist peacefully.*

between mountains. As a result, suitable panda habitat on one mountainside was separated from the habitat on another mountain. Pandas now live in about twenty isolated patches of forest throughout the mountains.[8]

The 70-square-mile (181-square-kilometer) Qianfoshan Nature Reserve is an island completely surrounded by people. An estimated fifteen to twenty-five pandas live in this reserve. At one time, a forested corridor connected this island refuge with panda habitat to the north, but the corridor has become farmland. The small panda population is completely isolated.[9]

▷ Poaching

Pandas have been under the protection of China's central government, at least on paper, since 1947. In 1963, laws made it illegal to hunt pandas. In 1989, the Chinese government passed the Wild Animals Protection Act. Under the terms of this act, people caught hunting an animal protected by the government face long prison terms. Others have been sentenced to life imprisonment, and some have been executed, for smuggling the skins of protected animals.

Unfortunately, the prices some people will pay for these illegal animal skins motivate poachers to

Animal Bytes: Giant Panda#Photos#Photos#Photos#Photos - Microsoft Internet Explorer

File   Edit   View   Favorites   Tools   Help

Address http://www.sandiegozoo.org/animalbytes/t-giant_panda.html#Photos   ↗Go

SAN DIEGO ZOO.org

| animal bytes home | reptiles | birds | insects | mammals | amphibians |

Quick facts

▣ Video Byte:
Giant Panda

SAN DIEGO
ZOO
video
click button to play

▣ Photo Bytes

Cla
(Ma

Mammals: Giant Panda

Range: southwestern China, in six small forest fragments

Habitat: damp, misty forests of bamboo and conifers, in altitudes above 4,000 feet (1,200 meters)

Giant pandas are black and white and loved all over

The giant panda is a national

**San Diego Zoo:
Animal Bytes**

The San Diego Zoo conducts pioneering research in giant panda reproduction at its own facility and in China with conservation biologists there. At the zoo's Web site, learn more about pandas and the people who are dedicated to saving them.

EDITOR'S CHOICE

Access this Web site from http://www.myreportlinks.com

risk the severe penalties. Panda pelts have sold for more than $10,000.[10]

Pandas sometimes die in snares intended for other animals. Male musk deer, which share panda habitat, have a gland that contains musk oil. This oil is used to make perfume, and it is also used in Chinese medicine. The money a poacher can get for one musk gland is a strong incentive for poaching. Sometimes just putting meat on the table is enough incentive.

Poachers' traps strangled two female pandas within four months while zoologist George Schaller studied giant pandas in the Wolong Reserve. One of the females, named Han-Han, wore a radio collar so that researchers could track her activity. Based on tracking information, Schaller suspected she had given birth not long before she died, but her baby would not have been old enough to survive on its own.[11]

In the Qinling Mountains to the north, seven pandas were lost to poachers in a fourteen-year period.[12] In Schaller's view, inbreeding is not the greatest danger facing pandas, since he is concerned that poaching might eliminate pandas first.[13]

Bamboo Die-off

Because pandas live almost entirely on chosen species of bamboo, periods of bamboo die-off can be a threat. Bamboo grows from rootlike stems

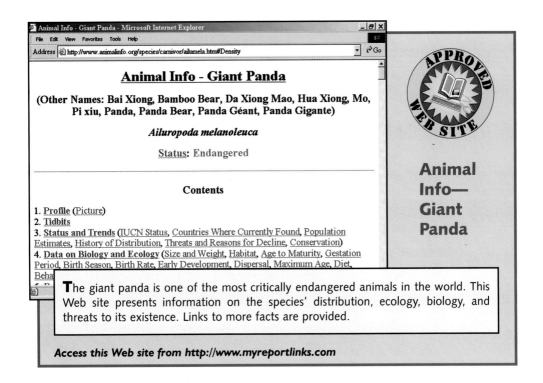

Animal Info—Giant Panda

that spread underground and send up new shoots each spring. Periodically all of a bamboo species in an area flower and die all at once, spreading millions of seeds. This mass flowering may happen once every several years or once in a hundred years, depending on the type of bamboo. Once the bamboo has died, it takes years before it has grown enough to support a panda population.

In the past, pandas faced with bamboo die-off simply moved to another area to choose another kind of bamboo. In fact, bamboo die-offs may have helped pandas by encouraging them to move to new territories and find new mates. As panda habitats have become fragmented, pandas have become less able to move to different areas. Future bamboo die-offs may cause isolated populations to starve.

Slow Reproduction

The survival of giant pandas as a species is also threatened by the slow reproductive rate of pandas combined with high infant mortality. In the wild, female pandas raise a single cub once every two or three years—if they are fortunate. Infant pandas develop slowly, which makes them vulnerable to predators and disease for a longer time. Researcher Pan Wenshi estimated that 40 percent of infant pandas die soon after birth.[14]

Chapter 4

PANDA RESEARCH BEGINS

When the World Wildlife Fund (WWF) came into being in 1961, its organizers looked for a symbol that would be easily recognized and embraced by the public. A giant panda named Chi-Chi had recently arrived at the London Zoo, and the organizers decided that her appealing face and distinctive black-and-white markings were just what they needed.[1] However, the WWF and other organizations had no opportunity to get involved in panda conservation in 1961. China was closed to outsiders.

▷ Dark Days for Pandas

In 1949, the Chinese revolutionary leader Mao Zedong unified his enormous country and began a series of programs intended to make it stronger. Unfortunately, Chairman Mao paid no attention to the effects his programs would have on China's ecology. The decades that followed were not good ones for the giant panda.

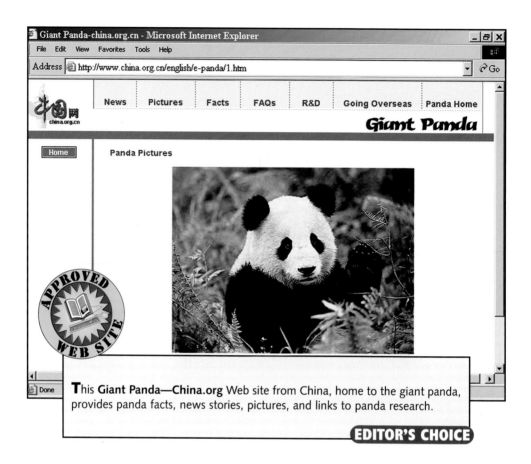

Giant Panda-china.org.cn - Microsoft Internet Explorer

File Edit View Favorites Tools Help

Address http://www.china.org.cn/english/e-panda/1.htm

News   Pictures   Facts   FAQs   R&D   Going Overseas   Panda Home

Giant Panda

Home   Panda Pictures

Done

This **Giant Panda—China.org** Web site from China, home to the giant panda, provides panda facts, news stories, pictures, and links to panda research.

EDITOR'S CHOICE

First, Mao encouraged families to have children. More people, he thought, would mean more energy and enthusiasm.[2] Later he instituted the Great Leap Forward. To make China more industrialized, Mao urged people to smelt steel everywhere they could build a furnace. Millions of trees became fuel for backyard furnaces. Farmers tended the furnaces instead of their crops—until famine struck. Following the famine, Mao urged everyone to plant grain, and people chopped down more trees to make more space for planting.

More people and fewer trees were not a good combination for giant pandas. As pandas traveled down the mountains to feed on bamboo shoots in the spring, they must have heard the axes chopping down trees.

The news was not all bad for pandas, however. The first nature reserves were established in 1958. The first panda reserves followed in 1963. Unfortunately, the reserves were not patrolled or protected. People could live, work, and chop down trees in these "protected areas" without even knowing that the land was set aside as a nature reserve.

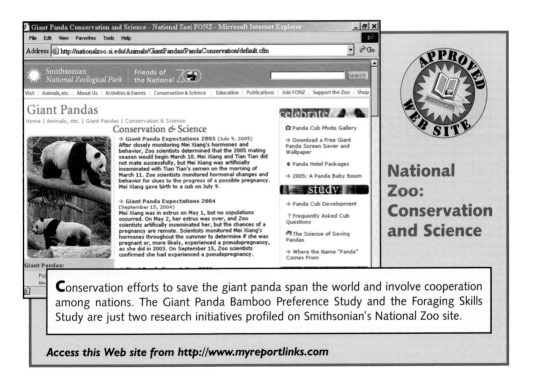

National Zoo: Conservation and Science

Conservation efforts to save the giant panda span the world and involve cooperation among nations. The Giant Panda Bamboo Preference Study and the Foraging Skills Study are just two research initiatives profiled on Smithsonian's National Zoo site.

Access this Web site from http://www.myreportlinks.com

▷ An Opening Door

In 1971, China's closed doors seemed to open a crack when the Chinese government invited the United States table-tennis team to China. Zoologist George Schaller immediately wrote letters to Chinese officials and to the World Wildlife Fund to suggest a study of giant pandas. It would be years before the partnership he suggested began to take shape.

The next year, United States president Richard Nixon visited China to establish official relations between the United States and China. As a gesture of goodwill, Chairman Mao gave the president two pandas, Ling-Ling and Hsing-Hsing. The pandas arrived at the Smithsonian Institution's National Zoo in Washington, D.C., in 1972.

Although the giant panda had been a symbol of friendship and goodwill since about A.D. 600 when a Chinese emperor gave two pandas to Japan, the Chinese knew little about the elusive pandas. To find out exactly how many giant pandas ambled through the fog-draped mountains, the Chinese government began a census. In April 1975 and again in May 1976, about three thousand people trudged through the mountains of central China to count pandas. Their findings suggested that about eleven hundred giant pandas lived in six separate locations.

▶ Panda Research Begins

In 1979, China invited members of the World Wildlife Fund to begin negotiating a joint WWF-Chinese effort to save the giant panda from extinction. Finally, George Schaller could study pandas. However, it soon became clear to Schaller that what Chinese officials really wanted was a research center to be built with Western money and filled with Western scientific equipment.[3]

In May 1980, after the WWF agreed to build a $1 million research facility, Schaller walked for

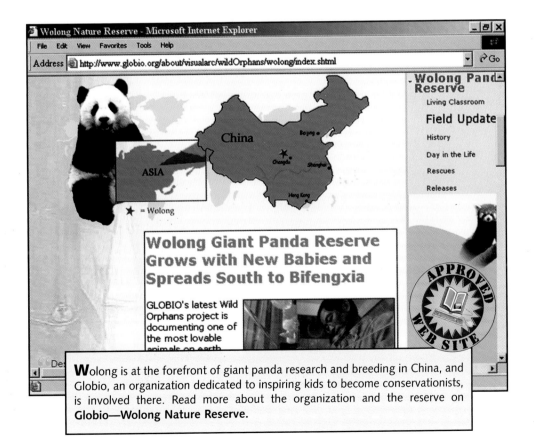

Wolong is at the forefront of giant panda research and breeding in China, and Globio, an organization dedicated to inspiring kids to become conservationists, is involved there. Read more about the organization and the reserve on Globio—Wolong Nature Reserve.

the first time in giant panda habitat. Later that year, he began his research with a team of Chinese researchers at the Wuyipeng research station in the Wolong Nature Reserve. At an elevation of 8,300 feet (2,530 meters), the Wuyipeng research station was usually cold and damp. Tents for sleeping and a communal hut for shared meals offered small comfort.

Days in the field were challenging. Researchers were often soaked to the skin as they struggled up the steep slopes. Actual sightings of pandas were very rare. Still, Schaller and the Chinese team continued with their work, trying to find answers to their many questions, such as how much food and what kind of food pandas require, and how much space they need to survive.

Gathering Information

Because researchers rarely saw pandas, they decided to capture a few of the animals and fit them with special collars so that they could monitor the animals' movements. The collars had radio transmitters that sent two signals: The transmitters beeped at seventy-five pulses each minute when the animal was resting and at one hundred pulses per minute when the animal was active. A receiver with a directional antenna could indicate the location of the collared panda. Since the radio signals could not pass through mountains, researchers needed to climb to the crest of a ridge to monitor them.

In December 1980, the team built four log traps and set ten snares. Meat was used as bait for the traps and snares. Although the black-and-white bears spend their time finding and eating their favorite bamboo, they do like meat when it is set in front of them.

For months, pandas avoided the traps. As Schaller noted, the traps were placed "with impeccable logic . . . where pandas ought to pass, on ridges and trails and in valley bottoms. However, human logic is not necessarily panda logic."[4] The traps had to be checked every day, and the snares checked twice each day. Meanwhile, the conservationists followed panda tracks and analyzed panda droppings to learn what they could about pandas.

▶ Contact

Finally, in March 1981, a young panda stepped in a snare. After researchers sedated the panda, they measured him, weighed him, and fitted him with a collar. Based on his size, they estimated his age at about two and a half years old. He was 54 inches (137 centimeters) from the tip of his nose to the end of his tail, and he weighed 120 pounds (54 kilograms). The team decided to locate the panda once a day and to record his activity for five whole days every month. Two days later, a 190-pound (86-kilogram) adult female entered one of the log traps, and she, too, was measured, weighed, and fitted with a collar.[5]

Eventually the team monitored five radio-collared pandas. The collars allowed the researchers to measure the home range of each panda and to learn when each animal was active and when it was resting. They learned that pandas are most active between 4 A.M. and 6 A.M. and then again between 4 P.M. and 7 P.M.[6] The researchers also learned that pandas eat different species of bamboo and different parts of the bamboo plant at different times of the year.

In 1984, Schaller helped Chinese conservationists establish another research station at Tangjiahe in the Min Mountains of northern Sichuan. Schaller left China in early 1985, and the work he had begun seemed to come to a stop for a time at both the Wuyipeng research station and the research station in Tangjiahe. The expensive facility in Wolong was neglected. Nevertheless, the pioneering work of Schaller and his team provided valuable knowledge about the behavior of wild pandas.

A Second Study

In 1985, Pan Wenshi, a Chinese scientist who had worked with Schaller, began a second study of wild pandas in the Qinling Mountains of Shaanxi Province. During the early years of his studies, he and his team of researchers paid their own expenses and lived on a modest diet of rice and potatoes.[7]

▲ Conservation plans to protect panda habitat have been implemented for less than two decades, so it remains to be seen whether pandas like this one will ultimately survive to roam China's forests.

A panda cub and trainer at the Chengdu Panda Breeding and Research Base.

The Qinling research team received permission in 1987 to capture pandas and fit them with radio collars. Eventually the researchers taught several radio-collared pandas to be comfortable with humans. When the pandas continued doing what they would normally do instead of quietly disappearing, researchers could watch panda behavior in the wild. One time they saw a mother panda bring her cub a toy—an old metal washbasin.[8] One of Pan's most remarkable achievements was his installation of a video camera inside a birth den—he was able to record, for the first time, a wild mother panda caring for her cub.

A Conservation Plan

In 1989, the WWF finished a giant panda conservation management plan based on George Schaller's research. The document stressed that the greatest threat to pandas was loss of habitat due to farming, logging, hunting, and grazing of livestock.

The WWF plan suggested that certain steps be taken to protect and restore the forests where pandas lived. One recommended step was relocating people who lived inside the boundaries of reserves. One such relocation had already been accomplished in the panda reserve at Tangjiahe. There, the Chinese Forestry Ministry provided money to help three hundred people, making up sixty families, move to nearby communities.

The plan proposed that logging be banned in parts of panda habitat and reduced in other parts so that the forest canopy could shelter bamboo and so that the forest could reseed itself naturally. It also called for native trees and bamboo to be planted in areas where habitat had been destroyed completely. It further stressed the need for trees and bamboo to be planted in a way that would connect forested areas so that pandas could travel from one area to another.

Other proposed actions included antipoaching patrols and better management of captive pandas to produce a self-sustaining breeding population. At the same time, the plan emphasized that wild pandas should not be caught for captive breeding.[9]

The WWF giant panda conservation management plan became the basis for a ten-year conservation plan approved by the Chinese government in 1992. China budgeted $13 million for the work the plan required and looked for another $64 million from conservation organizations and zoological societies outside China to carry it on.[10]

PANDAS FOR A PRICE

In 1984, as George Schaller began work at the panda research station in Tangjiahe, pandas took on a new role: These goodwill ambassadors became moneymaking commodities. Zoos from around the world began to compete against each other to "rent" pandas.

▶ From Ambassadors to Moneymakers

The giant panda's role as a goodwill ambassador for China began almost fifteen hundred years ago when Emperor Wu Zetian sent two giant pandas to Japan. In 1941, the government of Nationalist China gave two giant pandas to the Bronx Zoo in New York. During the 1950s, China's Communist government sent pandas to Moscow, the capital of the former Soviet Union, another Communist country. After giving Hsing-Hsing and Ling-Ling to the United States, China quickly sent panda "ambassadors" to Japan, France, England, Spain, Germany, and Mexico. By 1983, China had given twenty-four pandas to nine countries as a token of friendship.[1]

Then, in 1983, China stopped sending pandas as gifts. Instead, the government sent pandas on short-term loans—for a hefty price. The panda rentals began with two pandas loaned to the Los Angeles Zoo in 1984 as part of the Olympic Games celebration. The pandas stayed in Los Angeles for three months and then were sent to the San Francisco Zoo for another three months. San Francisco paid for the panda visit. The price was high, but the zoo made a profit through admission fees.

▶ Clamoring for Pandas

Suddenly, zoos across North America and Europe wanted to "rent" pandas. Between 1984 and 1987, pandas were sent to zoos in New York, San Diego, and Toronto, as well as Busch Gardens in Florida. Zoos in Japan, the Netherlands, Ireland, and Australia also exhibited pandas "borrowed" on short-term loans.[2] The zoos paid $50,000 per month to rent one panda, $100,000 per month for two. Additional costs included bringing Chinese personnel with the pandas sent to other countries. The increase in admissions more than offset the rental fees as people flocked to the zoos to see the pandas, but conservationists were worried about what the rental process was doing to the pandas themselves. What price were the pandas paying, removed from their natural habitat and relocated, if only temporarily, to countries all over the world?

Pandas in Court

By 1988, the United States Fish and Wildlife Service (FWS) learned that as many as thirty zoos and other institutions were negotiating with China for giant panda loans.[3] Political figures, including former first lady Nancy Reagan and former president Jimmy Carter, assisted with negotiations.[4]

That year, the World Wildlife Fund office in the United States and the American Zoo and Aquarium Association filed suit against the FWS for failing to enforce international regulations that applied to endangered species. (It was the responsibility of the FWS to evaluate requests to import pandas into the country and then issue permits.)

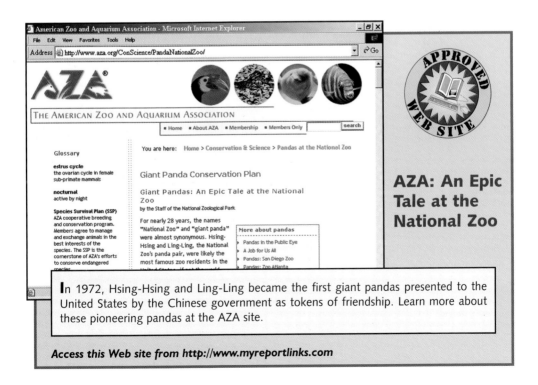

In 1972, Hsing-Hsing and Ling-Ling became the first giant pandas presented to the United States by the Chinese government as tokens of friendship. Learn more about these pioneering pandas at the AZA site.

Access this Web site from http://www.myreportlinks.com

The WWF and the AZA argued that the FWS was issuing permits without concern for the welfare of pandas.

Why would the zoo association take the issue of panda loans to court when so many of its members wanted them? What was wrong with the short-term visits? As Terry Maple, former director of Zoo Atlanta wrote, "Certainly the public enjoyed them, visiting in record numbers wherever pandas appeared."[5]

▶ International Protection

During the twentieth century, conservationists around the world became concerned about the

The IUCN-World Conservation Union Red List is a searchable database of the world's endangered animals and plants. A summary of each species listed on its Web site includes information on habitats and major threats.

Access this Web site from http://www.myreportlinks.com

rate at which species of all kinds were becoming extinct. In 1948 they came together to form the International Union for the Protection of Nature (IUPN). The organization changed its name in 1956 to the International Union for the Conservation of Nature and Natural Resources (IUCN). That name was shortened in 1990 to IUCN–The World Conservation Union.

In 1963, the IUCN began work on a treaty to protect endangered species. Ten years later, representatives of eighty countries, including the United States, signed the treaty, which was titled the Convention on International Trade in Endangered Species of Wild Fauna and Flora (CITES). That same year, the United States Congress passed the Endangered Species Act of 1973, to protect endangered species in the United States and internationally.

According to CITES, animals are not to be traded between countries if the purpose of the trade is primarily to make money. The only acceptable reasons for trade in endangered animals, according to CITES and the Endangered Species Act, are scientific research and increasing the species' chances of survival in the wild.[6] The IUCN listed the giant panda as an endangered species in 1984. That was the same year that China began sending pandas abroad for a fee, where they earned huge amounts as exhibits.

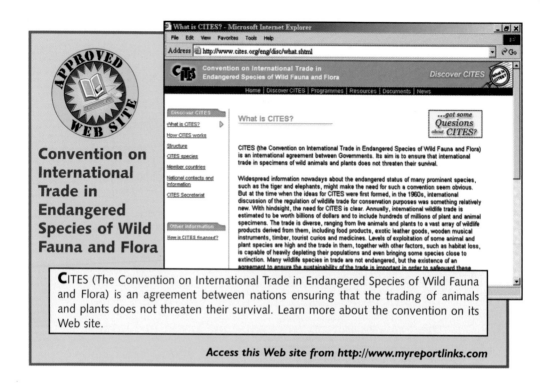

Access this Web site from http://www.myreportlinks.com

CITES (The Convention on International Trade in Endangered Species of Wild Fauna and Flora) is an agreement between nations ensuring that the trading of animals and plants does not threaten their survival. Learn more about the convention on its Web site.

The Role of Zoos

Zoos argued that the panda loans did enhance the survival of the species—in addition to bringing money to the zoos. After all, zoos educate people about animals, including rare animals. Zoos raise awareness of the need to protect endangered species. In addition, the large rental fees were sent to China for use in panda conservation.

However, the zoos had no control over the money when it reached China. WWF concluded that not all of the money went to conservation, and the money that did go directly to panda conservation may not have been spent wisely. George

Schaller pointed out that $120,000 from the zoo in Antwerp, Belgium, and $600,000 from the New York Zoological Society were used to build a panda breeding facility, although a panda breeding facility already existed nearby.[7] As Schaller wrote, "If the millions of dollars that have been raised from loans were spent on anti-poaching and forest protection measures instead of on the construction and maintenance of walls around pandas, the future of the species would be brighter."[8]

A Question of Numbers

At the heart of the objections to the short-term panda loans is the slow reproduction rate of pandas in the wild and high infant-mortality rate. A wild female panda will not have a cub until she is about five years old. Then she might have one infant every two to three years. If the mother panda lives a full life of twenty years, she may successfully raise only four cubs. At that rate, increasing the total number of pandas is a slow process. With so few wild pandas still surviving in the mountains, taking even one to visit zoos cannot be justified.

Efforts to breed pandas in captivity were not very successful until recently. According to the FWS, during a period of about fifty years, 345 captive pandas produced only 32 panda cubs that survived more than a year.[9] Sending an adult female panda on an international tour when she might, instead, become pregnant seemed to be sacrificing potential long-term benefit for short-term gain.

Zoos suggested that they exhibit only captive pandas that were not able to breed. The Chinese government made an effort to follow these guidelines and abide by the CITES regulations. However, the government did not always have control over which pandas were sent on tour. In the scramble to provide pandas to all the zoos that wanted them, young captive females and wild-caught females were sent abroad for exhibition.[10]

▶ Competing Agencies

Part of the problem in China was that two separate agencies competed to rent pandas. One agency, the Ministry of Forestry, was primarily responsible for the panda reserves and research stations. The other, the Chinese Association of Zoological Gardens, was primarily responsible for pandas in zoos.

In 1993, the FWS announced that it would not issue import permits for giant pandas until it could evaluate its policy regarding these permits. A new policy was completed in 1998. While the FWS was deciding to study its policy regarding giant panda imports, the AZA put together an "active

▲ The "rent-a-panda" phenomenon that sent giant pandas to zoos throughout the world has evolved into a more closely monitored program designed to help pandas breed successfully in captivity.

conservation strategy" for cooperation between North American zoos and Chinese colleagues. The Giant Panda Conservation Act Plan proposed to help the Chinese protect wild pandas in reserves and to develop an international master plan for breeding captive pandas.[11]

Panda Parents

While zoos around the world rushed to rent giant pandas, two zoos cooperated to produce a panda cub. During the 1970s, China gave two pandas to Mexico, where they lived in the Chapultepec Zoo. This pair mated and produced three offspring, the first surviving panda cubs to be born outside of China. When the Chapultepec Zoo looked for a mate for the pandas born at the zoo, the London Zoo offered its male panda, Chia-Chia. Chia-Chia's trip to Mexico included a stopover at the Cincinnati Zoo in Ohio, where he was exhibited for three months. The money raised during this stopover went to the Chapultepec Zoo to pay for expansion of its panda facilities. In 1990, Chia-Chia became a father.

THE ROLE OF ZOOS

When the United States Fish and Wildlife Service published its new policy on giant panda imports, it outlined requirements that zoos and other institutions would need to meet in order to receive an import permit. The new policy stated that giant pandas should be imported only for scientific purposes, to increase the number of pandas by breeding them, or to increase the species'

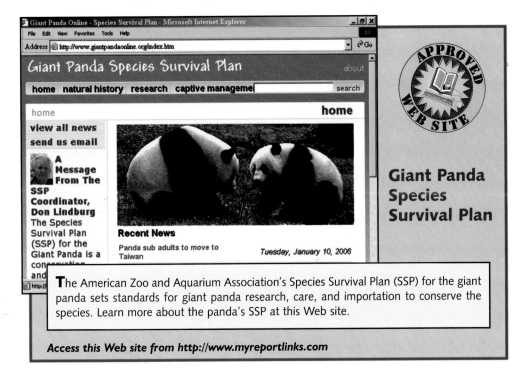

The American Zoo and Aquarium Association's Species Survival Plan (SSP) for the giant panda sets standards for giant panda research, care, and importation to conserve the species. Learn more about the panda's SSP at this Web site.

Access this Web site from http://www.myreportlinks.com

chances for survival in the wild. The new policy also suggested that all institutions with captive pandas should "cooperate in one international plan."[1]

The FWS policy also stated that most of the money sent to China in return for the pandas should be used for wild panda conservation. In addition, the institution applying for the permit would need to include a detailed budget showing exactly how the money would be spent.[2] However, some conservationists still believed that panda loans could actually help pandas survive.

The Scientific Loan

The San Diego Zoological Society had applied for a panda loan before FWS decided to stop issuing permits. As the FWS began to develop its new policy, Dr. Donald G. Lindburg, an anthropologist and zoo biologist with the San Diego Zoological Society's Center for Reproduction of Endangered Species (now Conservation and Research for Endangered Species, or CRES), worked with others at the San Diego Zoo to develop a new kind of panda loan. The San Diego plan proposed to increase knowledge about the giant panda and the number of captive pandas through captive breeding.

In 1996, the pandas Bai Yun and Shi Shi arrived at the San Diego Zoo to begin a twelve-year loan. In return, the San Diego Zoological Society agreed to contribute $1 million per year to China.[3] In addition, members of the San Diego team began joint research projects with Chinese scientists. Lindburg and another scientist from San Diego traveled to China to work with Chinese

Political Animals

Access this Web site from http://www.myreportlinks.com

Learn more about the politics, conservation, and economics of current international giant panda projects. Information on San Diego's "rented" pandas is included.

scientists at the China Research and Conservation Center for the Giant Panda at the Wolong Reserve. There the team gathered more information about pandas' use of scent markings to communicate.[4]

▷ Hua Mei

Much of the research scientists do to increase pandas' chances for survival progresses slowly behind the scenes. There is one area of research, though, that is producing dramatic results that people love to see.

Scientists are researching methods of improving artificial insemination in pandas. In artificial insemination, a syringe is used to inject a male's semen into the female's uterus. For reasons that scientists do not yet fully understand, captive pandas often choose not to mate. Since conservationists hope to develop a self-sustaining captive population, the unwillingness of pandas to breed in captivity is a problem. Artificial insemination is one solution.

At the San Diego Zoo, artificial insemination paid off quickly. In August 1999, Bai Yun gave birth to a female cub named Hua Mei. This cub was the first surviving cub born in the United States. When she was four years old, Hua Mei returned to China. (One condition of the long-term loan is that panda cubs born to the loaned pandas belong to China.) Soon after returning to China, Hua Mei gave birth to twins.

In 2003, Bai Yun gave birth to another cub named Mei Sheng. A third cub, Su Lin, followed in 2005.[5]

http://www.liu.edu/cwis/cwp/library/exhibits/panda/000114a.jpg - Microsoft Internet Explorer

File   Edit   View   Favorites   Tools   Help

Address   http://www.liu.edu/cwis/cwp/library/exhibits/panda/000114a.jpg   Go

Done

Hua Mei was born to Bai Yun at the San Diego Zoo in 1999. This image of mother and cub was taken four months later. Follow Hua Mei's development from birth to age three at the **Long Island University Library: Baby Panda!** Web page.

Zoo Atlanta

Zoo Atlanta in Georgia also developed a long-term panda research program in partnership with Chinese conservationists. In 1999, the giant pandas Lun Lun and Yang Yang arrived at a specially prepared panda exhibit area. Like the San Diego Zoo, Zoo Atlanta poured thought, imagination, and money into a comfortable home for the giant pandas that would allow for research and excellent viewing opportunities for visitors. The $7 million panda exhibit includes air-conditioned units to keep the pandas comfortable in the hot Atlanta summers and sixteen panda-cams to allow viewing twenty-four hours a day.[6]

According to its former director, Zoo Atlanta "specializes in the science of environmental enrichment."[7] Live plants, natural surfaces, and things to climb on are part of the enriched environment. The pandas play with movable objects and explore puzzle feeders to find food.

Another Research Plan

Like CRES's plan in San Diego, Zoo Atlanta's research plan covers a variety of topics, including how pandas react to play objects, puzzle feeders, and other stimulating parts of their environment. One important topic of study is panda socialization. Working with China's Chengdu Zoo and the Chengdu Research Base of Giant Panda Breeding, scientists connected with Zoo Atlanta are also looking at how pandas learn to be adults and parents.[8]

As the Zoo Atlanta specialists study pandas' social behavior, they consider the length of time young pandas stay with their mothers. In Chinese breeding centers, panda cubs are separated from their mothers at four to six months of age. This practice is meant to increase the chances that females will become pregnant again. However, scientists have found that wild panda cubs stay with their mothers two to three years. To learn more about the mother-cub relationship, scientists have allowed several young pandas at the

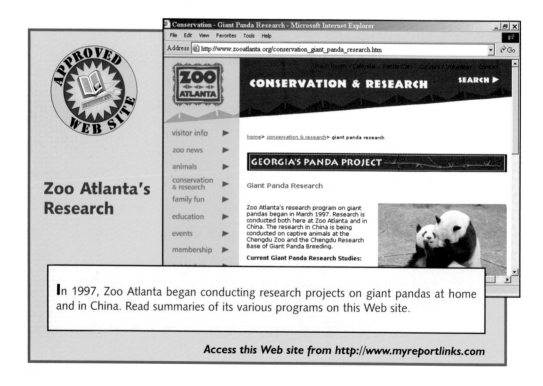

Zoo Atlanta's Research

In 1997, Zoo Atlanta began conducting research projects on giant pandas at home and in China. Read summaries of its various programs on this Web site.

Access this Web site from http://www.myreportlinks.com

Chengdu Research Base to stay with their mothers for more than a year.[9]

Conservationists had believed pandas to be solitary animals. Captive pandas, therefore, were often kept apart. However, when Pan Wenshi and Lu Zhi of Peking University studied pandas in the wild, they noticed that one young panda spent hours following and watching an older male. Perhaps, as the former Zoo Atlanta director suggests, "Pandas may not be so solitary after all."[10]

More Pandas and More Research

Other zoos in the United States have pursued the long-term loan-and-research plan. The National Zoo in Washington, D.C., was home to the two pandas given to the United States in 1972. But Ling-Ling died in 1992, and Hsing-Hsing was twenty-eight when he died in 1999. The National Zoo quickly developed a long-term plan and in December 2000 received Mei Xiang and Tian Tian. In July 2005, after being artificially inseminated, the National Zoo's Mei Xian gave birth to a cub, later named Tai Shan, adding one more to the number of captive pandas.

The National Zoo

The National Zoo, like the San Diego Zoological Society and Zoo Atlanta, spends $1 million each year on conservation in China, where the money is used to improve underdeveloped giant panda reserves. An additional $300,000 to $400,000 is devoted to research at the National Zoo and in China as well as training for individuals involved in panda conservation.[11]

Several times a year, scientists from the National Zoo, which has the largest department of reproductive sciences of any zoo in the world, travel to the Chengdu Base of Giant Panda Breeding and the China Conservation and Research Center for the Giant Panda in the Wolong Reserve to work with Chinese scientists. While the focus of the shared research is improved breeding among captive pandas, areas of study include nutrition, health, and psychological well-being. [12]

Information gained from scientific research is shared not only between the National Zoo and Chinese breeding centers but among other researchers in the United States as well. The benefits of the research are clear. In 1998 when scientists from the National Zoo began studying reproduction among captive pandas, there were 104 captive pandas in China. In 2005 the number was 142.[13]

▷ Success at Wolong

Wolong's breeding program is the most successful by far, however. Chinese researchers there have been able to both increase the pregnancy rate and

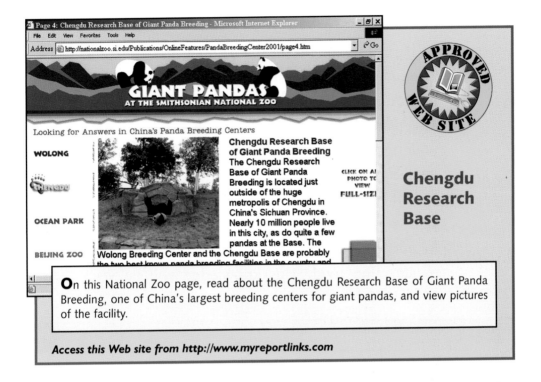

Page 4: Chengdu Research Base of Giant Panda Breeding - Microsoft Internet Explorer

File   Edit   View   Favorites   Tools   Help

Address http://nationalzoo.si.edu/Publications/OnlineFeatures/PandaBreedingCenter2001/page4.htm   Go

GIANT PANDAS
AT THE SMITHSONIAN NATIONAL ZOO

Looking for Answers in China's Panda Breeding Centers

WOLONG

CHENGDU

OCEAN PARK

BEIJING ZOO

Chengdu Research Base of Giant Panda Breeding
The Chengdu Research Base of Giant Panda Breeding is located just outside of the huge metropolis of Chengdu in China's Sichuan Province. Nearly 10 million people live in this city, as do quite a few pandas at the Base. The Wolong Breeding Center and the Chengdu Base are probably the two best known panda breeding facilities in the country and

CLICK ON A
PHOTO TO
VIEW
FULL-SIZE

**Chengdu
Research
Base**

On this National Zoo page, read about the Chengdu Research Base of Giant Panda Breeding, one of China's largest breeding centers for giant pandas, and view pictures of the facility.

Access this Web site from http://www.myreportlinks.com

improve the cubs' chances of survival once born. The Wolong team accomplished this in part by coming up with the idea of swapping twin cubs— taking one and placing it in an incubator while the other stayed with its mother, and then continually switching them—in an effort to save both. And researchers from the San Diego Zoological Society working at Wolong produced an improved infant formula to keep cubs alive and healthy. They also taught the Wolong researchers to use scent to find compatible pairs for mating. In 2005, there were sixteen surviving cubs at Wolong, compared with only two or three in all of the other breeding facilities in China.[14]

▶ A Focus on Nutrition

As part of its long-term panda loan, the Memphis Zoological Society in Tennessee developed a research plan that focused on panda nutrition. The plan involves seven research projects to be undertaken by fifteen scientists from five academic institutions and one giant panda reserve, supported by zoo staff.[15] By analyzing the ways that captive pandas choose food, the researchers hope to add to the understanding of the ways wild pandas find food. This knowledge will be very

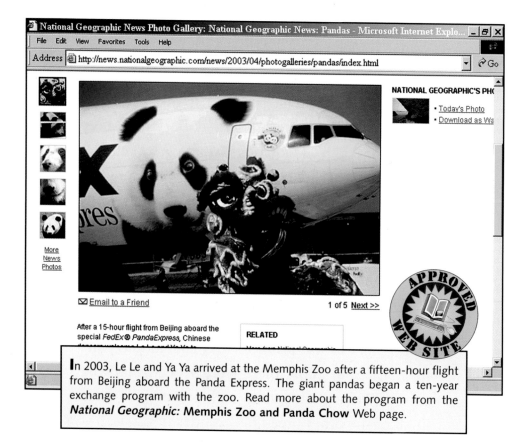

In 2003, Le Le and Ya Ya arrived at the Memphis Zoo after a fifteen-hour flight from Beijing aboard the Panda Express. The giant pandas began a ten-year exchange program with the zoo. Read more about the program from the *National Geographic:* **Memphis Zoo and Panda Chow** Web page.

helpful as conservationists restore habitat for wild pandas. The pandas Le Le and Ya Ya arrived at the Memphis Zoo in 2003 to begin a ten-year loan.

Benefits of Long-Term Loans

An obvious benefit of the long-term panda loans is that millions of Americans have opportunities to see giant pandas. Long-term loans are also proving to have long-term benefits for pandas.

In the few years since the long-term loans began, researchers have already gathered important information about pandas, and their research continues. Dr. Lindburg estimated that the four pairs of pandas in United States zoos in 2003 have participated in eighty research projects.[16] In addition, millions of dollars are going to China to help pandas survive in the wild.

China's Captive Pandas

When George Schaller first visited a Chinese panda-breeding facility in the early 1980s, he found an open-sided shed where pandas were kept in small, cold cells.[17] In 2001, David Powell, a scientist with the Smithsonian's National Zoological Park, visited two Chinese breeding facilities and found very different conditions. At the China Research and Conservation Center for the Giant Panda in the Wolong Reserve, Powell found large outdoor enclosures that he described as "literally enclosed forests with many climbing trees, thick undergrowth, steep terrain, and naturally growing bamboo."[18] This renovation came about after the Wolong staff had begun a six-month rotation at the San Diego Zoo in 1996, where they were able to witness pandas flourishing in modern zoo habitats.

The Chengdu Research Base of Giant Panda Breeding has been described as a huge "beautifully landscaped park."[19] When the weather gets warm, pandas find relief in indoor areas kept cool with large fans or air conditioning.

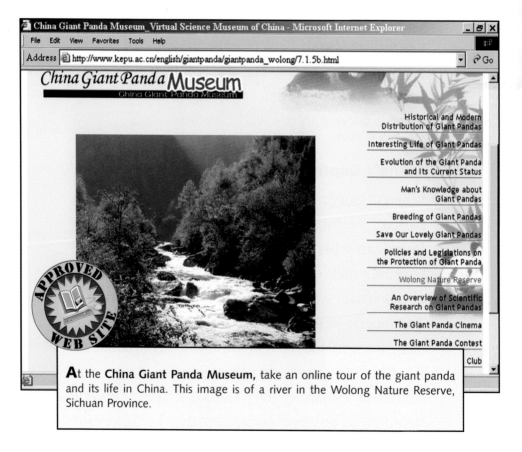

At the **China Giant Panda Museum,** take an online tour of the giant panda and its life in China. This image is of a river in the Wolong Nature Reserve, Sichuan Province.

▲ *The mountains of Sichuan Province, home to both people and pandas.*

▶ Experiments in Captive Breeding

Both Wolong and Chengdu are experimenting with methods to increase captive breeding, and their experiments have met with success. The Chengdu facility keeps females together for much of the year to see if that helps with their socialization. At the Wolong facility, females live in large outdoor enclosures where they can scent-mark trees. Then, zookeepers bring the females into smaller enclosures and release males into the outdoor areas to investigate the females' scent markings. Some of China's captive pandas live at the Beijing Zoo, which is also studying ways to encourage captive pandas to breed. The first panda cub born in captivity was born at the Beijing Zoo in 1963. But the Beijing Zoo, like most other captive-breeding facilities in China, has not had great success in panda births or cub survival.

Chapter 7

ON THE EDGE OF EXTINCTION

China recognized the value of the giant panda in 1949 when the government of the People's Republic of China designated the animal a national treasure. China's constitution stated that pandas and several other species should be protected.[1] Meaningful protection, however, was slow in coming.

▷ Protecting a National Treasure

In 1963, three areas were designated as panda reserves, and the hunting of pandas was prohibited by law. By the 1980s, thirteen nature reserves included panda habitat.[2] As George Schaller discovered, though, panda reserves do not necessarily offer protection for pandas or their habitat.

The Wolong Nature Reserve is one of China's oldest and largest reserves with habitat for giant pandas. The 772-square-mile (2,000-square-kilometer) reserve was established in 1975 as the panda reserve by which all others would be measured. An estimated 10 percent of all giant pandas live within its boundaries.

▲ *Reserves like the one at Wolong have helped make this panda's survival possible.*

In 2001, ecologist Liu Jianguo and a team of researchers published a study showing that destruction of giant panda habitat had increased within the reserve's boundaries after the reserve was established. Habitat destruction was actually greater inside the reserve than outside it.[3]

People and Pandas

This happened because people as well as pandas live in the Wolong Nature Reserve. In 1995, more than four thousand people in more than nine hundred households were living in the reserve.[4] These people are farmers. They clear land to plant crops, chop down trees to build homes, and raise animals that need to graze. The government persuaded three hundred people living in the Tangjiahe Reserve to relocate to a nearby town. Removing people from the reserve proved to be beneficial to the habitat. The government also tried to persuade the people of Wolong to relocate to nearby communities or to parts of the reserve where they would have less effect on the panda habitat. But the people of Wolong chose not to move.

The solution to this conflict between pandas and people may be education. After talking with people in the reserve, Liu concluded that older people preferred to stay in Wolong but liked the idea that their children might leave to go to college. Using computer simulations, Liu estimated that if 22 percent of the young people in Wolong left to attend college or take other jobs, the number of people living in the reserve would drop from forty-three hundred to seven hundred by 2047. However, if the situation continues on its course, about six thousand people would live in the reserve by 2047—and the habitat for pandas would be reduced by 40 percent.[5]

Money for Panda Reserves

The 1980s brought real change to panda conservation in China. The World Wildlife Fund and the Smithsonian National Zoological Park sent money and expertise to China. Those contributions helped

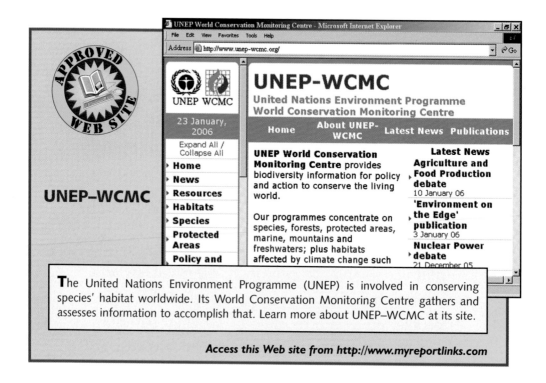

The United Nations Environment Programme (UNEP) is involved in conserving species' habitat worldwide. Its World Conservation Monitoring Centre gathers and assesses information to accomplish that. Learn more about UNEP–WCMC at its site.

Access this Web site from http://www.myreportlinks.com

lay the groundwork for cooperation between Chinese and Western conservationists that is producing exciting results in the twenty-first century. In 1992, China approved an ambitious ten-year conservation plan and allocated $13 million to carry out its provisions.

The long-term loan programs that began in the 1990s provide more money and a framework for more cooperative research, and China continues to establish new panda reserves. In 2005, more than fifty reserves covering more than 3,000 square miles (7,770 square kilometers) offered some protection for about two thirds of the giant panda population.[6]

▶ Tangjiahe

In 2001, Smithsonian National Zoological Park Director Lucy Spelman and others from the National Zoo visited China to see how money over the long term should be spent. One stop was the Tangjiahe Giant Panda Reserve in the Min Mountains of northern Sichuan. When George Schaller established the research station at Tangjiahe in 1984, an abandoned logging camp served as the reserve's headquarters. Seventeen years later, the headquarters included offices, a lecture hall, a natural history museum, staff residences, a guesthouse, a dining area, and even a

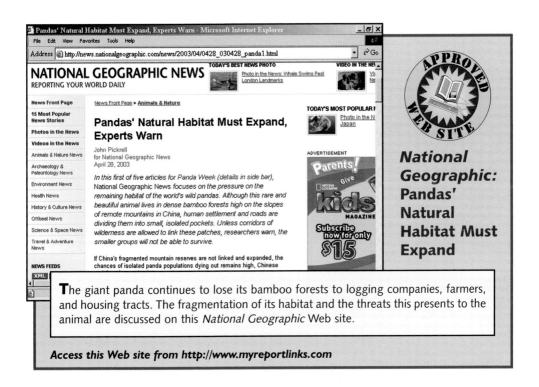

National Geographic: Pandas' Natural Habitat Must Expand

The giant panda continues to lose its bamboo forests to logging companies, farmers, and housing tracts. The fragmentation of its habitat and the threats this presents to the animal are discussed on this *National Geographic* Web site.

Access this Web site from http://www.myreportlinks.com

dance hall. A new education center was under construction.[7]

Even more impressive than the buildings are the community development projects that reduce the effects of human activities in the reserve. Tangjiahe helped build a hydroelectric power plant, which may help reduce the local population's use of wood for fuel. While the hydroelectric plant may help pandas in the long term, it does disrupt the forest. The dam covers acres of land with water, and the road to the dam cuts through the landscape.

The Tangjiahe Reserve is also helping local people earn money from activities that do not have a negative effect on the panda habitat, such as planting walnut and chestnut trees as a cash crop, beekeeping, and growing medicinal plants.[8]

By 2001, about ten thousand people a year were paying the equivalent of four dollars each to visit Tangjiahe. Plans call for increasing the size of the 154-square-mile (399-square-kilometer) reserve to include all the remaining panda habitat in the county.[9]

▷ **Yele Nature Reserve**

By contrast, Yele Nature Reserve, established in 1993, lacked just about everything when the National Zoo conservationists visited it in 2001. The reserve's protection station had no running

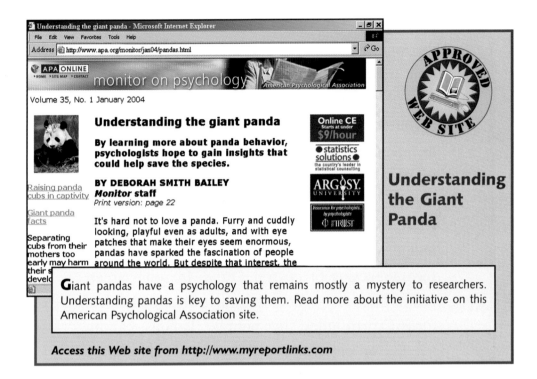

Understanding the giant panda - Microsoft Internet Explorer

File   Edit   View   Favorites   Tools   Help

Address 🔲 http://www.apa.org/monitor/jan04/pandas.html   ⟳ Go

APA ONLINE
▶HOME ▶SITE MAP ▶CONTACT

monitor on psychology   American Psychological Association

Volume 35, No. 1 January 2004

Understanding the giant panda

By learning more about panda behavior, psychologists hope to gain insights that could help save the species.

BY DEBORAH SMITH BAILEY
Monitor staff
Print version: page 22

It's hard not to love a panda. Furry and cuddly looking, playful even as adults, and with eye patches that make their eyes seem enormous, pandas have sparked the fascination of people around the world. But despite that interest, the

Online CE
Starts at under
$9/hour
● statistics
solutions ●
the country's leader in
statistical counseling

ARGOSY.
UNIVERSITY

Insurance for psychologists...
by psychologists
⟨I⟩ ℡TRUST

Raising panda cubs in captivity

Giant panda facts

Separating cubs from their mothers too early may harm their s... devel...

Understanding the Giant Panda

Giant pandas have a psychology that remains mostly a mystery to researchers. Understanding pandas is key to saving them. Read more about the initiative on this American Psychological Association site.

Access this Web site from http://www.myreportlinks.com

water and occasional electricity. To make a phone call, the reserve's staff had to travel thirty minutes to the nearest town. A new headquarters with offices, an education center, and staff housing was built, but it is located about two-and-a-half hours by car from the reserve.[10] The Yele Reserve also has a new dam and hydroelectric plant.

In its lack of basic supplies, Yele is like many of China's recently established reserves, but money from panda loans is bringing modern technology and infrastructure to the reserves. While establishing nature reserves demonstrates China's commitment to protecting its rare animals, birds, and plants, the reserves do not necessarily provide protection for the rare species within their boundaries. In fact, the Smithsonian team was surprised to see that no signs marked the boundaries of one new reserve.

Fragmented Habitat

As people clear land for crops, build dams and roads, and cut down trees, they divide panda habitat into smaller and smaller chunks. In 2005, conservationists estimated that pandas lived in about twenty isolated patches of forest throughout the mountains of central China. In some areas, fewer than ten pandas may live in an island of forest surrounded by people. Pandas cannot survive for long in such a fragmented habitat. One solution is to connect panda reserves with forested corridors that will allow pandas to travel from one reserve to another, and those corridors have become a focus of conservationists' efforts. At the same time, the country continues to develop quickly. As conservationists plan corridors, people are building roads and dams.

A Study Leads to Action

In 2000, the World Wildlife Fund–US, the World Wide Fund for Nature–China, and the Giant Panda Conservation and Research Center at Peking University in Beijing conducted a study of panda habitat in the Qinling Mountains at the northern end of panda habitat. Conservationists

Quick actions by the Chinese government in recent years have preserved more panda habitat, saving the home of this cub and others.

estimate that 220 pandas live in these mountains, but the population is separated into small groups by human activities in the mountains. The study showed fragmented habitat that would most likely doom small panda populations to extinction. But it also showed that nature reserves covered less than 50 percent of forested land suitable for pandas. The study called for three new reserves and several corridors to link patches of habitat.

The Chinese government took the study seriously and acted quickly. By 2003 it designated five new reserves and five new habitat corridors. In addition, a decision was made to bypass a busy mountain road that cut right through the best panda habitat. A tunnel now takes traffic through the mountain instead of over it.[11] The tunnel is good news for pandas, because the high mountain road will no longer be used.

▶ The People Connection

As the study of the Wolong Reserve showed, a growing human population can cause problems for pandas. China has adopted a policy of one child per family to control the growth of its enormous population. But many of the people living close to the pandas' mountain homes are members of China's ethnic minorities, and China's one-child policy does not apply to them. As this population continues to grow, conservationists are looking for ways to help local people earn a living without destroying panda habitat.

Many of these people made a living as loggers before logging was banned in the reserve in 1998. Conservationists hope that ecotourism, which will bring tourists into Wolong to see the pandas—and perhaps buy local products—will provide people with opportunities to earn a living without harming the forests. By helping local people earn money from tourism, conservationists hope to make the forests important to them.

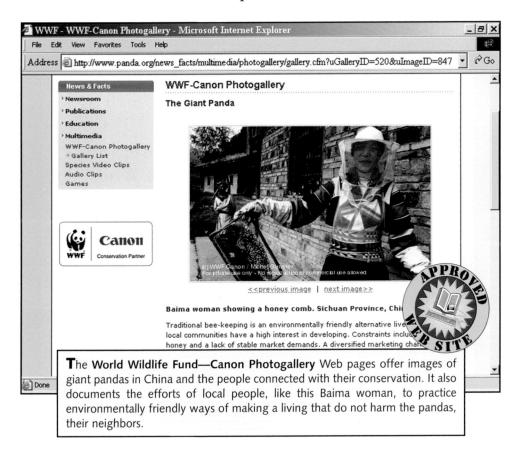

The **World Wildlife Fund—Canon Photogallery** Web pages offer images of giant pandas in China and the people connected with their conservation. It also documents the efforts of local people, like this Baima woman, to practice environmentally friendly ways of making a living that do not harm the pandas, their neighbors.

▶ Ecotourism

Since 1997, tourism in the Wanglang Nature Reserve in northern Sichuan has increased dramatically. About one thousand tourists visited the 124-square-mile (320-square-kilometer) reserve in 1997. About twenty thousand people visited the reserve in 2002.[12]

Most of the people who live close to the Wanglang Nature Reserve belong to the Baima people, a minority population. Early in the twenty-first century, some of the Baima people began opening their homes to tourists. Wearing traditional clothing, they entertain tourists with traditional customs and music. The World Wildlife Fund also arranged small-business loans so that women could make traditional items, such as tablecloths, to sell to tourists.

Ecotourism may increase the standard of living among people who live close to pandas. A study by the Chinese government indicated that tourism could bring up to $42 million per year to the Wolong Reserve.[13]

While conservationists hope ecotourism will help preserve the pandas' habitat, they recognize that ecotourism brings problems of its own. Too many tourists can damage the environment the tourists have come to see. Increased tourism means that roads need to maintained, and the tourists need places to stay and food to eat. Those

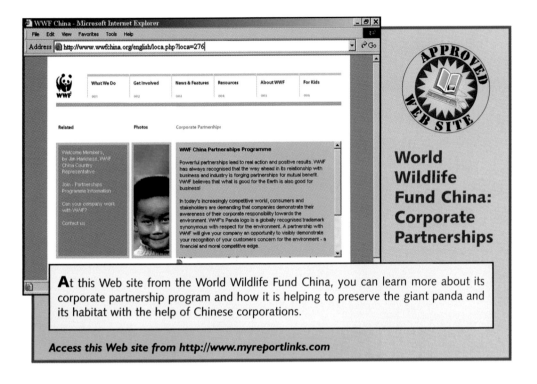

At this Web site from the World Wildlife Fund China, you can learn more about its corporate partnership program and how it is helping to preserve the giant panda and its habitat with the help of Chinese corporations.

Access this Web site from http://www.myreportlinks.com

needs must be balanced with the need to protect the preserves' inhabitants themselves.

▷ Beekeeping

Beekeeping is another promising alternative to logging. The World Wildlife Fund taught former loggers new beekeeping techniques. The beekeepers sell honey to the tourists. In addition, they sell honey to Carrefour, Europe's largest retailer and a member of WWF China's Corporate Partnership Programme. In other villages, farmers grow walnuts and Chinese peppers that they sell to Carrefour.[14]

The commitment and caring of conservationists has helped save many species, including the giant panda. But it is also vital that ordinary people participate in panda preservation, if the species is to survive.

A Future for Pandas

Each year, millions of dollars are spent to prevent the extinction of the panda, which has become the icon for endangered species around the world. If money can buy a future for the panda, then perhaps the species has a chance at survival in the wild. The Chinese government continues to demonstrate its commitment to the panda's survival.

However, conservation efforts will have to keep up with the demands of an enormous population. More than a billion people live in China, and many are poor. Millions of people reaching for a higher standard of living compete with about sixteen hundred pandas for the remaining natural resources in the mountains of central China.

Hope for the Species

Despite these challenges, the beginning of 2006 brought hopeful news for the future of China's national treasure. A Chinese newspaper reported in early January that twenty-one surviving baby pandas were born in Chinese zoos and breeding centers in 2005—surpassing the old record, set in 2003, of fifteen.

Of the captive pandas born in China in 2005, sixteen were born at the Wolong Giant Panda Research Center, and the rest were born in Chengdu, at Luoguantai in Shaanxi Province, and at the Beijing Zoo. According to Na Chunfeng, a State Forestry Administration official, "Despite the early deaths of a few baby pandas, 2005 has witnessed the largest number of surviving newborn pandas in China's history of artificial fertilization on the rare species."[15] Improved breeding techniques, money dedicated to conservation, and the commitment of researchers from China and abroad have all helped in the fight to save the endangered giant panda. But it is also the commitment and caring of ordinary people, young and old alike, to saving endangered species and preserving their habitat that will make the ultimate difference.

In 1973, Congress took the farsighted step of creating the Endangered Species Act, widely regarded as the world's strongest and most effective wildlife conservation law. It set an ambitious goal: to reverse the alarming trend of human-caused extinction that threatened the ecosystems we all share.

Each book in this series explores the life of an endangered animal. The books tell how and why the animals have become endangered and explain the efforts being made to restore their populations.

The United States Fish and Wildlife Service and the National Marine Fisheries Service share responsibility for administration of the Endangered Species Act. Over time, animals are added to, reclassified in, or removed from the federal list of Endangered and Threatened Wildlife and Plants. At the time of publication, all the animals in this series were listed as endangered species. The most up-to-date list can be found at **http://www.fws.gov/endangered/wildlife.html.**

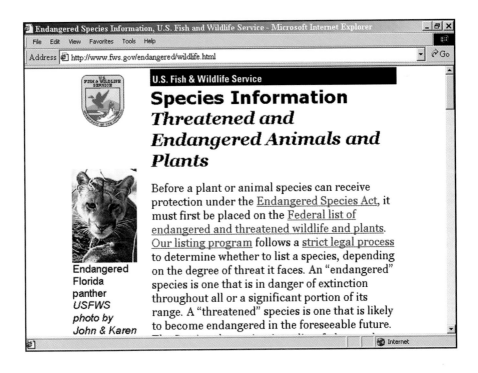

Report Links

The Internet sites described below can be accessed at http://www.myreportlinks.com

▶**Smithsonian National Zoological Park**
Editor's Choice Visit the resident giant pandas at the National Zoo.

▶**Giant Panda—WWF**
Editor's Choice The giant panda symbolizes the WWF's conservation efforts.

▶**ARKive: Giant Panda**
Editor's Choice View images of pandas at this Web site.

▶*Nature: Bamboo Bears*
Editor's Choice PBS covers the birth of a giant panda in captivity.

▶**San Diego Zoo: Animal Bytes**
Editor's Choice Learn about pandas from the San Diego Zoo.

▶**Giant Panda—China.org**
Editor's Choice A Chinese site provides an overview of China's national treasure.

▶**American Embassy: Panda Primer**
The United States Embassy in China presents a panda primer.

▶**Animal Info—Giant Panda**
An overview of panda information is presented on this site.

▶**AZA: An Epic Tale at the National Zoo**
The American Zoo and Aquarium Association presents an epic panda tale.

▶**Chengdu Research Base**
Take a quick tour of the Chengdu Research Base of Giant Panda Breeding.

▶**China Giant Panda Museum**
At this site, learn about China's programs to save the giant panda.

▶**China's Biosphere Reserves**
Read about China's protected reserves on this UNESCO Web site.

▶**Convention on International Trade in Endangered Species of Wild Fauna and Flora**
This international agreement aims to stop the illegal trade in endangered species.

▶**ENN: Protecting China's National Treasure**
Read about the fight to save China's national treasure, the giant panda.

▶**Giant Panda Species Survival Plan**
Learn more about the AZA's Species Survival Plan for the giant panda.

Report Links

The Internet sites described below can be accessed at http://www.myreportlinks.com

▶**Globio—Wolong Nature Reserve**
Find out about Wolong from Globio, an international environmental organization for kids.

▶**International Network for Bamboo and Rattan (INBAR)**
The International Network for Bamboo and Rattan promotes sustainable development.

▶**IUCN Red List**
The IUCN Red List catalogues the world's endangered species.

▶**Long Island University Library: Baby Panda!**
View photos of Hua Mei, a panda born at the San Diego Zoo in 1999.

▶**MSU: Panda Habitat Research in China**
A university Web site offers research on pandas and their habitat.

▶*National Geographic:* **Memphis Zoo and Panda Chow**
A *National Geographic* story focuses on panda food at the Memphis Zoo.

▶*National Geographic:* **Pandas' Natural Habitat Must Expand**
This *National Geographic* article discusses giant panda habitats.

▶**National Zoo: Conservation and Science**
The Smithsonian's National Zoo examines the preservation of a much-loved animal.

▶**Political Animals**
This *San Diego Magazine* article examines the on-loan pandas of the local zoo.

▶**Understanding the Giant Panda**
The mystery of panda behavior is discussed in this article.

▶**UNEP–WCMC**
Learn about a United Nations organization that works to conserve species.

▶**USFWS Endangered Species Program Kids Corner**
This USFWS Web page offers ways you can help save endangered species.

▶**World Wildlife Fund—Canon Photogallery**
View images from China of giant pandas in their natural habitat.

▶**World Wildlife Fund China: Corporate Partnerships**
Learn about WWF's corporate partnerships in China that are helping to protect pandas.

▶**Zoo Atlanta's Research**
Zoo Atlanta offers this overview of giant panda research.

artificial insemination—The process of using a syringe to inject semen into a female's uterus.

calorie—A unit of measure for the energy (heat) that food provides.

canine teeth—The four pointed teeth toward the front of the jaws in many animals.

carnivores—Animals that eat meat. Cats, for example, are carnivores.

climate—The weather conditions in an area. These conditions include temperature, amount of precipitation (rain or snow), humidity (moisture in the air), and wind.

delayed implantation—The delay between the time a female egg is fertilized and the time the egg attaches itself to the wall of the uterus so that it can become a baby. The delay may be one month or as much as four months.

diet—The food normally eaten by an animal.

DNA (deoxyribonucleic acid)—A molecule that carries the genes that make the young of a species like its parents.

ecology—The relationship between living things and their environment.

ecotourism—The practice of visiting natural settings to see the rare plants and animals that live in that setting. Ecotourism is proving to be an effective way to make endangered species valuable to people who live near them. Tourists spend money when they visit, and their money helps the local economy.

evolution—A change in the gene pool from generation to generation. These changes may make an animal better at surviving in its habitat.

forest canopy—The leaves on trees that provide shade cover for plants growing beneath the trees.

genes—The basic physical units of heredity, which means that genes carry "instructions" so that a panda cub, for example, will grow up to be like its parents. Gene pool refers to the total genes in a population (such as pandas).

habitat—The natural environment of an animal that provides what the animal needs for survival, such as food and shelter.

herbivores—Animals that eat plants. Cows and horses are herbivores.

omnivores—Animals that eat both meat and plants.

radial sesamoids—The enlarged wrist bones on pandas' paws that are almost like thumbs and allow pandas to hold their food with their front paws.

radio collar—A collar with a tiny battery-operated transmitter that sends signals (usually beeps) that can be picked up by a receiver.

red panda—A small raccoonlike animal with cinnamon-red fur. The red panda shares the giant panda's habitat, and bamboo is its primary food. The red panda is more likely than the giant panda to add berries, seeds, and acorns to its diet.

rhizome—A rootlike stem that grows underground and sends out roots below ground as well as shoots that grow above ground.

scent posts—Trees or other objects that pandas mark with scent secreted by glands under their tails. Pandas may also claw the scent post or spray urine on it. Scent posts are an important means of communication among pandas.

temperate climate—A climate without extremes of cold or hot weather.

zoologist—A scientist who studies animals.

Chapter 1. In Love With Pandas

1. Staff, National Zoological Park, "Giant Pandas: An Epic Tale at the National Zoo," *The American Zoo and Aquarium Association,* n.d., <http://www.aza.org/Con Science/PandaNationalZoo/> (September 29, 2005).

2. Terry L. Maple, Ph.D., *Saving the Giant Panda* (Marietta, Ga.: Longstreet Press, 2000), p. 8.

3. "Census Finds More Giant Pandas in the Wild," *Smithsonian National Zoological Park,* June 2004, <http://national zoo.si.edu.cfm> (July 15, 2005).

4. Keith and Liz Laidler, *Pandas: Giants of the Bamboo Forest* (London: BBC Books, 1992), p. 12.

5. "Wolong's Temperate Forest," *Globio,* 2004, <http://www.globio.org/glossopedia/lpanda/LPTemperate Forest.html> (July 26, 2005).

6. Susan Lumpkin and John Seidensticker, *Smithsonian Book of Giant Pandas* (Washington, D.C.: The Smithsonian Institution, 2002), p. 98.

7. "Mammals: Giant Panda," *San Diego Zoo,* n.d., <http://sandiegozoo.org/animalbytes/tgiant_panda.html> (July 25, 2005).

8. George B. Schaller, *The Last Panda* (Chicago: University of Chicago Press, 1993), p. 62.

9. Lumpkin and Seidensticker, p. 19.

10. Schaller, pp. 262–264.

11. Maple, p. 2.

12. Schaller, p. 49.

13. Lumpkin and Seidensticker, p. 22.

14. Ibid.

15. Ibid., p. 25.

16. "Census Finds More Giant Pandas in the Wild," *Smithsonian National Zoological Park.*

Chapter 2. The Grass-Eating Bears

1. George B. Schaller, *The Last Panda* (Chicago: University of Chicago Press, 1993), p. 171.

2. Ibid., p. 97.

3. Tamar Simon, "Sex and the Captive Giant Panda," *Discovery Channel,* May 26, 1999, <http://www.exn.ca/Stories/1999/05/26/52.asp> (October 3, 2005).

4. "Plants: Species Collection: Bamboo," *San Diego Zoo,* n.d., <http://www.sanddiegozoo.org/CF/plants/collectiondetail.cfm?ID=3> (July 25, 2005).

5. Keith and Liz Laidler, *Pandas: Giants of the Bamboo Forest* (London: BBC Books, 1992), p. 65.

6. Susan Lumpkin and John Seidensticker, *Smithsonian Book of Giant Pandas* (Washington, D.C.: The Smithsonian Institution, 2002), p. 66.

7. Schaller, p. 103.

8. Ibid., p. 102.

9. Lumpkin and Seidensticker, p. 69.

10. Schaller, p. 73.

11. Ibid., p. 103.

12. Lumpkin and Seidensticker, p. 82.

13. Schaller, p. 101.

14. "Seasonal Influences on Chemical Communication in Giant Pandas," *San Diego Zoo,* n.d., <http://cres.sandiegozoo.org/projects/sp_season_comm_pandas.html> (October 3, 2005).

15. Lumpkin and Seidensticker, p. 82.

16. Don Lindburg, "Splendid Beauty Arrives in San Diego," *The American Zoo and Aquarium Association,* February 2000, <http://www.aza.org/ConScience/PandaSanDiego> (September 29, 2005).

17. Laidler, p. 142.

18. Lindburg.

19. Ibid.

20. "Captive Giant Panda Maternal Behavior," *Zoo Atlanta,* n.d., <http://www.zooatlanta.org/conservation_giant_panda_ research_maternal.htm> (October 6, 2005).

21. Ibid.

Chapter 3. An Uncertain Future

1. Susan Lumpkin and John Seidensticker, *Smithsonian Book of Giant Pandas* (Washington, D.C.: The Smithsonian Institution, 2002), p. 135.

2. Ibid., p. 6.

3. "Forests of the Upper Yangtze," *World Wildlife Fund,* n.d., <http://www.worldwildlife.org./wildplaces/fuy/index.cfm> (August 17, 2005).

4. Daniel Winkler, "Floods, Logging, and Hydro-Electricity; the Impact on Tibetan Areas," *Tibet Environmental Watch,* January 1, 1999, <http://www.tew.org/archived/china.floods.log.html> (October 10, 2005).

5. Lumpkin and Seidensticker, p. 147.

6. Keith and Liz Laidler, *Pandas: Giants of the Bamboo Forest* (London: BBC Books, 1992) p. 113.

7. Lumpkin and Seidensticker, p. 79.

8. Claire Doole, "Protecting China's National Treasure," *World Wildlife Fund,* September 5, 2005, <http://www.panda.org/about_wwf/what_we_do/species/stories/ news.cfm?uNewsID=22610> (September 6, 2005).

9. Lumpkin and Seidensticker, pp. 163–167.

10. Terry L. Maple, Ph.D., *Saving the Giant Panda* (Marietta, Ga.: Longstreet Press, 2000), p. 117.

11. George B. Schaller, *The Last Panda* (Chicago: University of Chicago Press, 1993), p. 123.

12. Martin Williams, "Scientist Who Fights for the Pandas," February 2000, <http://www.drmartinwilliams.com/panwenshi/ panwenchi.html> (October 6, 2005).

13. Schaller, p. 149.

14. Lumpkin and Seidensticker, p. 89.

Chapter 4. Panda Research Begins

1. "A History of WWF: The Sixties," *WWF,* n.d., <http://www.panda.org/about_wwwf/who_we_are/history/sixties.cfm> (September 22, 2005).

2. George B. Schaller, *The Last Panda* (Chicago: University of Chicago Press, 1993), p. 150.

3. Ibid., p. 12.

4. Ibid., p. 33.

5. Ibid., p. 56.

6. Susan Lumpkin and John Seidensticker, *Smithsonian Book of Giant Pandas* (Washington, D.C.: The Smithsonian Institution, 2002), p. 69.

7. Martin Williams, "Scientist Who Fights for the Pandas," February 2000, <http://www.drmartinwilliams .com/panwenshi/ panwenchi.html> (October 6, 2005).

8. Ibid.

9. Schaller, pp. 270–273.

10. Ibid., p. 281.

Chapter 5. Pandas for a Price

1. George B. Schaller, *The Last Panda* (Chicago: University of Chicago Press, 1993), p. 235.

2. Ibid., p. 237.

3. "Policy on Giant Panda Permits," *U.S. Fish and Wildlife Service, International Affairs,* p. 2, August 27, 1998, <http://www.fws.gov/international/fedregister/pandpoly .html.> (October 11, 2005).

4. Schaller, p. 237.

5. Terry L. Maple, Ph.D., *Saving the Giant Panda* (Marietta, Ga.: Longstreet Press, 2000), p. 17.

6. Schaller, p. 240.

7. Ibid., p. 239.

8. Ibid., p. 245.

9. "Policy On Giant Panda Permits," p. 7.

10. Schaller, p. 236.

11. David L. Towne, "Giant Panda Conservation Plan— Saving the Giant Panda: A Job for Us All," *The American Zoo and Aquarium Association,* February 2002, <http://www .aza.org/ConScience/PandaJob/> (October 10, 2005).

Chapter 6. The Role of Zoos

1. "Policy on Giant Panda Permits," *U.S. Fish and Wildlife Service, International Affairs,* p. 21, August 27, 1998, <http://www.fws.gov/international/fedregister/pandpoly .html.> (October 11, 2005).

2. Ibid., pp. 23–24.

3. "Giant Panda Birth News," *San Diego Zoo,* August 2, 2005, <http://www.sandiegozoo.org/news/panda_news _birth.html> (September 26, 2005).

4. Susan Lumpkin and John Seidensticker, *Smithsonian Book of Giant Pandas* (Washington, D.C.: The Smithsonian Institution, 2002), p. 8.

5. "Giant Panda Birth News," *San Diego Zoo.*

6. Terry L. Maple, Ph.D., *Saving the Giant Panda* (Marietta, Ga.: Longstreet Press, 2000), p. 94.

7. Ibid., pp. 78–79.

8. "Studying Atlanta's Pandas," *The American Zoo and Aquarium Association,* n.d., <http://www.aza.org/ ConScience/PandaZooAtlanta/> (October 17, 2005).

9. Ibid.

10. Maple, p. 67.

11. Lumpkin and Seidensticker, p. 26.

12. "Spotlight on Zoo Science: The Science of Saving Pandas," *Smithsonian National Zoological Park,* July 22, 2005, <http://nationalzoo.si.edu.cfm> (September 29, 2005).

13. Ibid.

14. Dr. Donald Lindburg, November 2005, comments as manuscript advisor.

15. Michael Pelton, "Memphis Zoological Society (MZS) Giant Panda *(Ailuropoda Melanoleuca)* Research Plan," *Memphis Zoo Conservation Action Network,* n.d., <http://www.memphiszoo.org/canpandas.html> (December 29, 2005).

16. John Pickrell, "At Memphis Zoo, Scientists Ponder Panda Chow," *National Geographic News,* April 30, 2003, <http://news.nationalgeographic.com/news/2003/04 /0430_030430_pandaresearch.html> (September 8, 2005).

17. George B. Schaller, *The Last Panda* (Chicago: University of Chicago Press, 1993), p. 8.

18. David M. Powell, "Looking for Answer in China's

Panda Breeding Centers," *Giant Pandas at the Smithsonian National Zoo,* 2001, <http://nationalzoo.si.edu/Publications /OnlineFeatures/PandaBreedingCenter2001/page3.htm> (July 29, 2005).

19. Ibid.

Chapter 7. On the Edge of Extinction

1. Keith and Liz Laidler, *Pandas: Giants of the Bamboo Forest* (London: BBC Books, 1992), p. 156.

2. "Census Finds More Giant Pandas in the Wild," *Smithsonian National Zoological Park,* June 2004, <http://national zoo.si.edu.cfm> (July 15, 2005).

3. Jianguo Liu, et al., "Ecological Degradation in Protected Areas: The Case of Wolong Nature Reserve for Giant Pandas," *Science,* vol. 292, April 6, 2001, <http://www.sciencemag.org> (September 26, 2005).

4. Ibid.

5. Susan Lumpkin and John Seidensticker, *Smithsonian Book of Giant Pandas* (Washington, D.C.: The Smithsonian Institution, 2002), p. 163.

6. Claire Doole, "Protecting China's National Treasure," *World Wildlife Fund,* September 5, 2005, <http://www .panda.org/about_wwf/what_we_do/species/stories/news .cfm?uNewsID=22610> (September 6, 2005).

7. Lumpkin and Seidensticker, p. 176.

8. Ibid., p. 175.

9. Ibid., p. 177.

10. Ibid., p. 171.

11. John Pickrell, "Pandas' Natural Habitat Must Expand, Experts Warn," *National Geographic News,* April 28, 2003, <http://news.nationalgeographic.com/news/2003 /04/0428_030428_panda1.html> (September 8, 2005).

12. "Ecotourism as an Alternative to Logging in Panda Habitat," *WWF,* June 20, 2003, <http://www,panda.org /news_facts/newsroom/other_news/news.cfm?uNewsID =7564> (October 12, 2005).

13. Tony Sutton, "Ecotourism: Panda's Paladin or Bane?" *Trade and Environment Database, Case Study Number 700,* 2003, <http://www.american.edu/TED/panda-tour.htm> (October 12, 2005).

14. Claire Doole, "Protecting China's National Treasure," *WWF.*

15. The Associated Press, "China says 21 rare pandas born in '05," *MSNBC.com,* January 3, 2006, <http://www .msnbc.msn.com/id/10682894/> (January 10, 2005).

Bortolotti, Dan. *Panda Rescue: Changing the Future for Endangered Wildlife.* Buffalo: Firefly Books, 2003.

Claybourne, Anna. *Giant Panda.* Chicago: Heinemann Library, 2005.

Cothran, Helen, ed. *Endangered Species: Opposing Viewpoints.* San Diego: Greenhaven Press, 2000.

Green, Carl. *The Giant Panda: A MyReportLinks.com Book.* Berkeley Heights, N.J.: MyReportLinks.com Books, 2004.

Lumpkin, Susan, and John Seidensticker. *Smithsonian Book of Giant Pandas.* Washington, D.C.: Smithsonian Institution Press, 2002.

Lü Zhi. *Giant Pandas in the Wild: Saving an Endangered Species.* New York: Aperture, 2002.

Maynard, Thane. *Working With Wildlife: A Guide to Careers in the Animal World.* New York: Franklin Watts, 1999.

Rain Forests of the World. New York: Marshall Cavendish, 2002.

Robinson, Phillip T. *Life at the Zoo.* New York: Columbia University Press, 2004.

Stone, Lynn M. *Giant Pandas.* Minneapolis: Carolrhoda Books, 2004.